OccupyMedia!

The Occupy Movement and
Social Media in Crisis Capitalism

OccupyMedia!

The Occupy Movement and
Social Media in Crisis Capitalism

Christian Fuchs

Winchester, UK
Washington, USA

First published by Zero Books, 2014
Zero Books is an imprint of John Hunt Publishing Ltd., Laurel House, Station Approach,
Alresford, Hants, SO24 9JH, UK
office1@jhpbooks.net
www.johnhuntpublishing.com
www.zero-books.net

For distributor details and how to order please visit the 'Ordering' section on our website.

Text copyright: Christian Fuchs 2013

ISBN: 978 1 78279 406 6

A CIP catalogue record for this book is available from the British Library.

Design: Stuart Davies

Printed in the USA by Edwards Brothers Malloy

We operate a distinctive and ethical publishing philosophy in all
areas of our business, from our global network of authors to
production and worldwide distribution.

CONTENTS

Other key works by Christian Fuchs

Fuchs, Christian. 2014. *Digital labour and Karl Marx*. New York: Routledge.

Fuchs, Christian. 2014. *Social media. A critical introduction*. London: Sage.

Trottier, Daniel and Christian Fuchs, eds. 2014. *Social media, politics and the state: Protests, revolutions, riots, crime and policing in the age of Facebook, Twitter and YouTube*. New York: Routledge.

Fuchs, Christian and Marisol Sandoval, eds. 2013. *Critique, social media and the information society*. New York: Routledge.

Fuchs, Christian and Vincent Mosco, eds. 2012. *Marx is back – The importance of Marxist theory and research for Critical Communication Studies today. tripleC: Communication, Capitalism & Critique* 10 (2): 127-632. http://www.triple-c.at/index.php/tripleC/issue/view/25

Fuchs, Christian, Kees Boersma, Anders Albrechtslund, Marisol Sandoval, eds. 2012. *Internet and surveillance. The challenges of web 2.0 and social media*. New York: Routledge. Routledge Studies in Science, Technology and Society Series.

Fuchs, Christian. 2011. *Foundations of critical media and information studies*. New York: Routledge.

Fuchs, Christian and Rainer E. Zimmermann. 2009. *Practical civil virtues in cyberspace: towards the utopian identity of civitas and multitudo*. Aachen: Shaker.

Fuchs, Christian. 2008. *Internet and society: social theory in the information age*. New York: Routledge.

Fuchs, Christian. 2005. *Herbert Marcuse interkulturell gelesen* (Herbert Marcuse read interculturally, in German). Interkulturelle Bibliothek Vol. 15. Nordhausen: Bautz.

Fuchs, Christian. 2005. *Emanzipation! Technik und Politik bei Herbert Marcuse* (Emancipaton!: Technology and Politics in the Works of Herbert Marcuse, in German). Aachen: Shaker.

"The goal-determining activity of capital can only be that of growing wealthier, i.e. of magnification, of increasing itself. [...] The labour which stands opposite capital is alien labour, and the capital which stands opposite labour is alien capital. The extremes which stand opposite one another are specifically different. [...] Where they relate to one another [...] negatively, as in the case of money, it becomes madness; madness, however, as a moment of economics and as a determinant of the practical life of peoples. [...] the real not-capital is labour".
—Karl Marx

This book is dedicated to the worldwide new working class of activists that struggles for justice and against capitalism.

Acknowledgement:

This work contains information from the OccupyMedia! Dataset that was collected and published as SPSS and CSV files, 2012/2013, available at: http://fuchs.uti.at/wp-content/Occupy Media!_Dataset.sav and http://fuchs.uti.at/wp-content/Occupy Media!_Dataset.csv under the Open Database License (ODbL) v1.0 http://opendatacommons.org/licenses/odbl/1.0/

The OccupyMedia! Survey's full questionnaire can be found at: http://fuchs.uti.at/wp-content/questionnaire.pdf

Rules and guidelines for the usage of the dataset: http://fuchs.uti.at/wp-content/DataUsageGuide.pdf

Description of the dataset: http://fuchs.uti.at/wp-content/ mapping_questions_variables.pdf

Thanks! I thank Susann Krieglsteiner and Taghrid Baba who helped me organizing the OccupyMedia! Survey's data collection.

Contact http://fuchs.uti.at @fuchschristian chris tian.fuchs@uti.at

1. Introduction: The Crisis of Capitalism

Voices of Occupy activists:

- *On capitalism*: "For me, the Occupy movement is one important part of the catalyst which will bring change to this corporate/political bloodsucking system that is bleeding us all dry" (#386).

- *On activism*: "My impression is that the growing population of young (20-30) people with very dissatisfying life situations (e.g. little work / debt), the increasingly disturbing political / social climate, and social media combined to create this new form of action" (#375).

- *On social media activism*: "Not everyone can go to the camps but the rest of us can help spread the word through social media" (#333). "Social media is then a good starting place for activism, but it can not end there, real action loud and in the streets is what works best!" (#259). "What awakened me. When I heard the 99% slogan, it all began to make sense. I had never been an activist before I heard about Occupy on Facebook. Now I am involved in Occupy ... every day, and have joined local peace groups and churches with their outreach programs for the poor. I am no longer alone or feel helpless. I am changing my world" (#275).

- *On social media surveillance:* Activists learned "the hard way about how closely monitored social media is by law enforcement on a local, state, and federal level. Occupy Austin was infiltrated by law enforcement agencies, resulting in serious legal problems for several participants" (#265).

- *On alternative social media*: "I would love to see activists using Diaspora and The Global Square, as they offer real advantages in terms of user privacy. However – until there is a critical mass of users, these forms of communications are redundant in organising mass protest, and only serve as a way of limited communication between organisers" (#238). "Yes, the majority of the people don't know of the existence of the alternative platforms or simply don't use them. It is necessary to use the commercial platforms to reach a maximum of society. There can be a difference in the sort of information sharing on the platforms, while the commercial ones are basically good for sharing the knowledge, showing people what goes around and sharing basic information for meet-ups, the alternative platforms that are more secure can be used for more specific or detailed information, strategy, group-building, creating a knowledge-database" (#127).

This book presents the results of a study of the Occupy movement's use of social media. It tells a story of social media activism, social media censorship and surveillance, corporate domination of social media and alternative social media in the context of the political economy of capitalism. The global crisis of capitalism forms the societal background of the Occupy movement and its media use. The causes of the crisis are explained in the introduction.

Section 2 gives an overview of the rise of social movements in contemporary crisis capitalism. Section 3 presents a classification of Occupy's use of digital media. Section 4 explains the methodological foundations of the OccupyMedia! Survey. Section 5 presents the survey's basic results that are interpreted in section 6. Section 7 draws conclusions about media activism in an antagonistic world.

This study is grounded in the approach of the critical political economy of communication that studies "the social relations, particularly the power relations, that mutually constitute the production, distribution, and consumption of resources, including communication resources" (Mosco 2009, 2). It analyses how the Occupy movement challenges power and in this context makes use of communication resources and how power structures and relations limit and pose potentials for this kind of communication.

The study presented in this work is grounded in the approach of the critical political economy of communication that studies "the social relations, particularly the power relations, that mutually constitute the production, distribution, and consumption of resources, including communication resources" (Mosco 2009, 2). The work at hand analyses how the Occupy movement tries to challenge power and in this context makes use of communication resources and how power structures and relations limit and pose potentials for this kind of communication.

Critical political economy analyses power structures and ideologies on the one hand and is on the other hand interested in praxis, "activity by which people produce and change the world" (Mosco 2009, 34). This means that the analysis of a phenomenon such as labour requires an understanding of the structural capital-labour relationship constituted by modes of surplus production and appropriation and at the same time insights into actual or potential labour struggles. "Social movements are particularly important for a political economy of communication because they have influenced the development of the means and content of communication. [...] Among the most prominent issues are how democratic should be the lines of internal communication, the extent to which a movement should adopt mainstream forms of external communication, and the degree of specialized or expert attention a movement should devote to media activity" (Mosco 2009, 204). Critical political economy is interested in class structures and ideological "incorporation and legitimation" just like it wants to uncover "gaps and contradictions" that constitute "cracks and fissures" that allow "currents of criticism and movements of contestation"

(Golding and Murdock 1978, 353).

Capitalism is a social form that is "incomplete and contradictory" (Garnham 1990, 36). This incompleteness and antagonistic structure is expressed in crises, struggles and social movements.

The work at hand contributes to the political economy of communication's task to analyse communication contradictions in capitalism by focusing on the Occupy movement's communication forms and strategies, their limits and potentials and especially the question of how corporate and alternative, non-commercial digital media enable and or/limit the movement's communication and protest capacities. The book aims to show that there is a political economy right at the heart of social movements' media use, a political economy that is constituted by power relations between corporate media and non-corporate media.

In recent years, scholars have given more attention to the question how knowledge producers work and struggle. The crucial question in this context is: "Will knowledge workers of the world unite?" (Mosco and McKercher 2008, 13). The Occupy movements around the world have made visible the deep division of contemporary capitalist societies in terms of class, gender, ethnicity and other lines of stratification. By making use of media, activists act as producers and diffusers of knowledge. At the level of social movement analysis, the question if knowledge workers of the world will unite relates therefore to the question if and how mediated protests can be networked and mutually support each other.

In 2008, a global crisis of the capitalist economy started. Neoliberalism has resulted in relative stagnation and wage losses, whereas profits have rapidly increased. Neoliberalism is a class struggle project of the ruling class aimed at increasing profits by decreasing wages with the help of strategies such as the deregulation of labor laws, precarious labor conditions, welfare and public expenditure cuts, tax cuts for the rich and companies, the privatization of public goods, the global offshoring and outsourcing of labor, etc. Many working families had to take out loans, consumer credits and mortgages in order to be able to pay for their everyday life requirements. At the same time, capital investment into high-risk financial instruments boomed because the growing profits needed to be reinvested. Workers' debts were packaged into new financial instruments, so-called Asset Backed Securities (ABS), Mortgage Backed Securities (MBS), Collateralized Debt Obligations (CDOs) and Credit Default Swaps (CDS). The financial market promised high financial gains, but the profits in the non-financial economy could in long run not fulfil these growth expectations, which created a mismatch between financial values and the profits of corporations and between the expectations of shareholders and the reality of capitalist accumulation. The results were financial bubbles that burst in the 2008 crisis.

Critical theories of the crisis do not agree what its exact structural causes are (see e.g. Duménil and Lévy 2011, Foster and McChesney 2012, Harvey 2010, 2011a, 2011b, Kliman 2012, Lapavitsas et al. 2012, McNally 2011, Resnick and Wolff 2010), but see it not as a failure of regulation, but as the outcome of capitalism's immanent fundamental contradictions:

1) The relative disparity between the rich and companies on the one hand and the mass of people on the other hand is an expression of the class antagonism between capital and labor.

2) The financialization of the capitalist economy is based on an antagonism between the fictitious value of financial capital and the actual profits that this capital achieves on the commodity markets, i.e. the antagonism between virtual/fictitious values and real values of capital.

3) A third dimension is what David Harvey (1990) has termed the overaccumulation of capital: The need to accumulate capital, the exploitation of labor and capital's technological progress and organizational dynamics tend to result in idle capital that is crisis-prone if it cannot find spheres of investment. The overaccumulation tendency is an antagonism between the production and consumption/investment of capital.

A crisis is the "manifestation of all the contradictions of bourgeois economy" (Marx 1863, book 2, chapter XVII). "The fact that the movement of capitalist society is full of contradictions impresses itself most strikingly ... in the changes of the periodic cycle through which modern industry passes, the summit of which is the general crisis" (Marx 1867, 103). Table 1 shows the annual growth of labor productivity since the early 1970s in the G7 countries (Canada, France, Germany, Italy, Japan, UK, USA) and the whole OECD.

The combined annual growth of labor productivity in the G7 countries was 88.0% in the years 1971-2011. This means that in 40 years productivity has almost doubled.

Year	G7	OECD	Year	G7	OECD
1971	4.0	N.A.	1992	2.7	N.A.
1972	4.8	N.A.	1993	1.7	N.A.
1973	4.3	N.A.	1994	1.8	N.A.
1974	1.7	N.A.	1995	1.4	N.A.
1975	2.2	N.A.	1996	1.9	N.A.
1976	3.4	N.A.	1997	2.0	N.A.
1977	2.7	N.A.	1998	1.8	N.A.
1978	2.8	N.A.	1999	2.6	N.A.
1979	2.1	N.A.	2000	2.9	N.A.
1980	0.8	N.A.	2001	2.0	1.8
1981	2.5	N.A.	2002	2.4	2.1
1982	0.9	N.A.	2003	2.0	2.1
1983	2.6	N.A.	2004	1.9	2.4
1984	2.6	N.A.	2005	1.5	1.7
1985	2.8	N.A.	2006	1.3	1.5
1986	2.0	N.A.	2007	1.2	1.7
1987	1.6	N.A.	2008	0.2	-0.1
1988	2.3	N.A.	2009	0.5	-0.3
1989	2.2	N.A.	2010	2.3	2.1
1990	2.5	N.A.	2011	1.5	1.5
1991	1.6	N.A.			

Table 1: Annual growth of labor productivity in the G7 and OECD countries, 1971-2011, data source: OECD iLibrary

Who has benefited from the strong productivity growth? In order to answer this question, we need to have a look at the development of the power relation between labor and capital. The rise of neoliberalism has been accompanied by a deregulation of financial markets, an encouragement of financial speculation and a massive redistribution of wealth from wages to profits. By class struggle from above, capital managed to increase its profits by relatively decreasing wages. The resulting profits were to a certain degree invested into financial markets and high-risk financial instruments, which increased the crisis-proneness, instability and volatility of capitalism. Comparing the years 1970 and 2013, the wage share, which is the share of wages in the GDP, decreased in the following way in selected European countries.

Country	2013	2007	2000	1990	1980	1970
EU15	58.4%	56.8%	58.9%	61.0%	65.7%	63.4%
Germany	58.6%	55.1%	60.6%	58.8%	63.7%	61.1%
Ireland	49.3%	50.3%	48.2%	59.4%	70.0%	67.2%
Greece	47%	53.5%	55.6%	62.4%	60.3%	64.8%
Spain	52.3%	55.3%	58.9%	60.7%	66.8%	64.2%
France	58.9%	56.8%	57.2%	59.3%	68.5%	63.0%
Italy	54.7%	53.7%	53.2%	61.9%	66.6%	65.4%
Cyprus	52.4%	55.0%	56.2%	N.A.	N.A.	N.A.
Portugal	55.6%	57.2%	59.2%	55.0%	66.7%	72.5%
United Kingdom	64.2%	61.9%	62.5%	65.0%	66.0%	65.5%
Finland	58.8%	53.7%	53.8%	63.5%	63.6%	63.1%
USA	58.2%	60.6%	63.2%	63.1%	65.1%	65.9%
Japan	61.0%	58.6%	64.4%	64.3%	72.8%	64.4%
Canada	55.1%	56.4%	56.4%	59.7%	59.3%	61.0%

Table 2: Adjusted wage share as percentage of GDP at current market prices, data source: AMECO

The data show that in the past 40 years, capitalist class struggle from above has resulted in a relative decrease of wages in many countries. This struggle has, in Europe especially, been intense in countries such as Greece, Spain, Ireland and Cyprus, where the wage share dropped from values around 65% in 1970 to values around 50% in 2013. But also the wages in almost all other European and many other countries were affected, although to different degrees. Wages in the USA, Japan and Canada were undergoing a similar development as in Europe.

How have profits developed in parallel with the relative fall of wages? Net operating surplus is a variable that measures the gross value added of an economy minus fixed capital investments minus wage costs minus corporate taxation. Calculating the share of net operating surplus in the value of the GDP gives an estimation of capital's net share in an economy's total wealth. Profit share = Net operating surplus / GDP

Tables 3, 4 and 5 show the development of the profit shares in the EU 15 countries, the UK and the USA.

Year	Net operating surplus (NOS), in billion €	GDP in current market prices, in billion €	Profit share
1975	321.3	1426.3	22.5%
1980	555.4	2537.8	21.9%
1990	1357.1	5449.1	24.9%
2000	2115.1	8760.3	24.1%
2007	2949	11531.8	25.6%
2008	2860	11478.6	24.9%
2009	2476.6	10876.9	22.8%
2010	2661.3	11332.9	23.5%
2011	2715	11650.6	23.3%
2012	2688.1	11898.9	22.6%
2013	2690.6	11990.7	22.4%

Table 3: The development of the profit share in the EU 15 countries (data source: AMECO)

Year	Net operating surplus (NOS), billion £	GDP in current market prices, billion £	Profit share
1975	15.8	106.9	14.8%
1980	36.9	233.7	15.8%
1990	115.4	574.1	20.1%
2000	203.6	975.3	20.9%
2007	335.7	1412.1	23.8%
2008	351.7	1440.9	24.4%
2009	309.9	1401.9	22.1%
2010	326.8	1466.6	22.3%
2011	339.5	1516.3	22.4%
2012	331.9	1546.2	21.5%
2013	335.4	1589.1	21.1%

Table 4: The development of the profit share in the UK (data source: AMECO)

Year	Net operating surplus (NOS), billion US$	GDP in current market prices, billion US$	Profit share
1975	351.1	1623.4	21.6%
1980	560.5	2767.5	20.3%
1990	1298.5	5754.8	22.6%
2000	2444.9	9898.8	24.7%
2007	3437.5	13961.8	24.6%
2008	3375.5	14219.3	23.7%
2009	3218.4	13898.3	23.2%
2010	3627	14419.4	25.2%
2011	3767.6	14991.3	25.1%
2012	4021	15589.6	25.8%
2013	4248.6	16123.5	26.4%

Table 5: The development of the profit share in the USA (data source: AMECO)

In 1980, the profit share was 20.3% in the USA, 15.8% in the UK and 21.9% in in the EU 15 countries. What followed was the rise of neoliberal politics in the USA and Europe. Thatcher came to power in the UK in 1979, Reagan in the US in 1981. There were close bonds between Thatcherism and Reagonomics in terms of ideology and political collaboration. Ten years later (in 1990), the profit share had risen to 22.6% in the USA, 20.1% in the UK and 24.9% in the EU 15 countries, whereas the wage shares had simultaneously decreased, which is an indication for successful neoliberal class politics that redistributed income from employees to companies and the rich. These developments further continued: in 2000 the profit shares increased to 24.7% in the USA, 20.9% in the UK and remained relatively constant in the EU 15 region as a whole. In 2007, a year before the crisis started, the profit share was 24.6% in the USA, 23.8% in the UK and 25.6% in the EU 15, whereas since 2000 the wage share had fallen by 2.1% USA, 0.6% in the UK and 2.6% in the EU 15 countries. In the period 1980-2007, the wage share decreased in these countries/regions by 4.5% (USA), 4.1% (UK) and 8.9% (EU 15), whereas the profit share increased by 4.3% (USA), 8.0% (UK) and 3.7% (EU 15). While capital had constantly high growth rates during the 1980s, 1990s and 2000s, wages stagnated or relatively declined. Neoliberalism increased the wealth of corporations at the expense of labor. In the USA, the profit share fell to 23.2% in 2009 as an effect of the crisis, but was at a high of around 26% in 2012 and 2013. In the EU 15 countries, high profit shares around 25% before the crisis were reduced to around 22-23% in the years after the crisis. In the UK, the profit share dropped from around 24% before the crisis to a level of 21-22% after the crisis.

The working class in many European and other countries was hit hard by austerity measures and a new round of neoliberalism in the aftermath of the crisis: The wage share decreased from 55% in 2007 (before the crisis) to 52.4% in 2013 in Cyprus, from 53.5% to 47% in Greece, from 52.9% to 49.6% in Hungary, from

70.1% to 62.2% in Iceland, from 50.3% to 49.3% in Ireland, from 53% to 46.4% in Latvia, from 49.7% to 44.1% in Lithuania, from 57.2% to 55.6% in Portugal and from 55.3% to 52.3% in Spain (data source: AMECO). In Poland and Slovakia, workers have already before the crisis been relatively poor: the wage shares were 46.5% in 2007 and 46.1% in 2013 in Poland. The respective values for Slovakia were 42.3% in 2007 and 43.1% in 2013.

Decreasing relative wages of employees increased the dependence of their families on consumer credits, loans and mortgages for financing basic needs such as housing and transport. In the Euro 17 countries, the gross debt-to-income ratio of households increased from 74.91% in 2000 to 87.6% in 2005, 94.96% in 2008 and 99.36% in 2011 (data source: Eurostat). In the UK, this value was 101.0% in 2000, 138.6% in 2005 and 155.34% in 2008 (ibid.). In the USA, the household debt increased from US$ 1396 billion in October 1980 to US$ 3571.6 billion in October 1990, US$ 6963.5 billion in October 2000, US$ 11716.4 billion in October 2005 and US$ 13711.6 billion in October 2007 (data source: Federal Reserve Economic Data, Household Credit Market Debt Outstanding). The class struggle of capital against the working class that resulted in falling wage shares and high profits has been accompanied by a decrease in corporate taxation. The available data on corporate taxation is relatively incomplete. In the EU 27 countries, corporate taxes accounted in 2013 for only 0.3% of the GDP. In the United States the value was 0%, meaning that treated as a collective capitalist, companies in the USA do not pay taxes. Table 6 shows some of the limited available data. It indicates that corporate taxation has since the 1970s in general been low in European and North American capitalism, never reaching up to 1% of the GDP of a country and varying in most countries between 0 and 0.3%. It is interesting to observe that in 1970 the UK (0.8%) and the USA (0.5%) taxed capital higher than Germany (0.1%) and the Netherlands (0.2%). The rise of neoliberalism has resulted in a subsequent lowering of corporate taxation in both the UK and the USA. Overall the data in table 6 shows that those who make European and North American tax regimes are friends of capitalist interests, which has supported the neoliberal class struggle of capital against labor.

	2013	2007	2005	2000	1995
Germany	0.2	0.2	0.2	0.1	0.1
Netherlands	0.3	0.3	0.3	0.4	0.3
Austria	0	0.1	0.1	0.1	0
Portugal	0	0	0	0.1	0.1
Finland	0.2	0.3	0.3	0.3	0.2
United Kingdom	0.2	0.3	0.2	0.2	0.2
United States	0	0.2	0.3	0.4	0.3
	1990	1985	1980	1975	1970
Germany	0.1	0.1	0.1	0	0.1
Netherlands	0.2	0.2	0.2	0.2	0.2
Austria	0.1	0.1	0.1		
Portugal	0.1	0.2	0.1		
Finland	0.2	0.1	0.1	0.1	
United Kingdom	0.2	0.3	0.2	0.3	0.8
United States	0.3	0.2	0.3	0.4	0.5

Table 6: Corporate taxes, percentage of GDP at market prices, data source: AMECO

The working class' wages have been attacked by neoliberal policies. The resulting profits were invested in finance because capital is driven by the need to accumulate ever more profits and financial speculation promised high returns. The volatility of the economy steadily increased, which resulted in a big explosion in 2008. The result was more of the same: hyper-neoliberalism, which means the intensification of neoliberalism. Banks were bailed out with taxpayers' money, which means a bailout by taxes predominantly paid by employees because companies hardly pay taxes. The discourse of austerity wants to make people believe that they have lived beyond their means, that austerity is necessary because states have spent too much money, etc. The circumstance that profits have been ever more growing, wages shrinking and that companies have hardly paid taxes is not mentioned in the dominant ideology. The working class has become more and more exploited by capital and the reaction to the crisis has been an intensification of exploitation and the attempt to legitimate this form of exploitation that works by redistribution of income from workers to companies, cuts of public expenditures, wage cuts, tax support for banks and companies with the help of the argument that states have spent too much money, etc. The working class is constantly being dispossessed of the wealth it produces. Austerity measures bring much more of the same. Banks have been bailed out with taxpayers' money in what can be described as politics of socialism for the rich. That many companies are hardly paying taxes is part of this politics. The described circumstances are at the heart of the crisis of the state. The intensification of neoliberalism makes capitalism and states even more volatile and increases inequalities. Rising profits resulted in the need to invest them in order to avoid an overaccumulation crisis. This circumstance spurred the financialization of capitalist economies. Table 7 shows the development of the share of the finance industry in the total value added of selected countries. A general increase can be observed that has been especially strong in the USA, where the share has doubled from 1970 until 2005, when it made up 8.1% of the US economy's total value added. The data indicates an increased financialization of capitalism.

	Canada	France	Germany	Italy
1970	5.3%	4.1%	3.4%	4.4%
1980	4.8%	4.5%	4.4%	5.7%
1990	6.0%	5.4%	4.8%	5.0%
2000	7.1%	5.1%	4.2%	4.7%
2005	7.4%	4.9%	4.7%	4.8%
2008	N.A.	4.6%	3.6%	5.3%
2009	N.A.	N.A.	4.3%	5.4%
	Japan	**UK**	**USA**	
1970	4.3%	N.A.	4.2%	
1980	5.2%	N.A.	4.9%	
1990	5.9%	6.6%	6.0%	
2000	5.8%	5.2%	7.7%	
2005	6.7%	7.1%	8.1%	
2008	5.8%	N.A.	7.7%	
2009	5.7%	N.A.	8.3%	

Table 7: Share of the financial industry in the total economy's value added (in current prices) of selected countries, data source: OECD iLibrary, STAN, financial industry=ISIC Rev. 3: C65-C67

Derivatives are high-risk financial instruments that derive their value from other assets. Over-the-counter derivatives are traded directly between two partners. They include instruments such as foreign exchange contracts, forwards and forex swaps, currency swaps, interest rate contracts, forward rate agreements, interest rate swaps, equity-linked contracts or credit default swaps. They are high-risk because they are not direct ownership titles, but depend on the value of other assets. Figure 1 shows the development of the share (in %) of the global gross market value of over-the-counter derivatives in world GDP. The share rapidly increased from around 10% in 2000 to 57.5% in 2008. It dropped after the start of the global capitalist crisis. The data show the tremendous growth of high-risk financial capital.

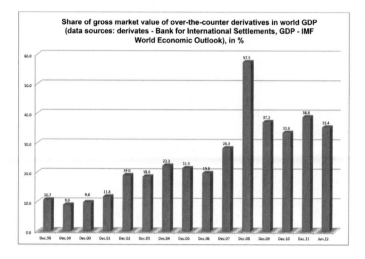

Figure 1: Share of the global gross market value of OTC derivatives in world GDP (in %)

The presented data shows that the capitalist economy has since the middle of the 1970s been shaped by the capitalist class' neoliberal struggle against the working class, increasing inequality between capital and labor, an increase of household debts, a decrease of corporate taxation, the rising financialization of the economy and as a consequence an increased vulnerability for crisis. The contradictions between capital and labor, fictitious value and actual profit, the production and consumption/ investment of capital were heightened by the development dynamics of neoliberal capitalism and finally resulted in a new world economic crisis.

2. Protests in Crisis Capitalism

2011 was a year of protests, revolutions and political change. It was a year where people all over the world tried to make their dreams of a different society a reality. There were revolutions in Tunisia and Egypt and Yemen, civil wars in Libya and Syria and the emergence of protests in countries such as Albania, Algeria, Armenia, Australia, Azerbaijan, Bahrain, Belarus, Belgium, Bolivia, Burkina Faso, Canada, Chile, China, Colombia, Czech Republic, Cyprus, Denmark, Djibouti, Finland, France, Georgia, Germany, Greece, Hong Kong, Hungary, India, Iran, Iraq, Ireland, Israel, Italy, Jordan, Kuwait, Lebanon, Macedonia, Malawi, Malaysia, Maldives, Mauritania, Mexico, Mongolia, Morocco, Netherlands, New Zealand, Nigeria, Norway, Oman, Palestine, Portugal, Russia, Saudi Arabia, Slovenia, Somalia, South Africa, South Korea, Spain, Switzerland, Sri Lanka, Sudan, Turkey, United Kingdom, United States, Vietnam, Western Sahara.

The Wikipedia entry http://en.wikipedia.org/wiki/Category:Protests_by_year gives a basic overview of important protests during the past years. It lists 2 protests in 2003, 1 in 2005, 12 in 2006, 18 in 2007, 13 in 2008, 22 in 2009, 24 in 2010, 76 in 2011, 46 in 2012 (accessed on April 22, 2013). If these data adequately reflect reality, then the temporal agglomeration of protests is an indication that 2011 was special, a tipping point, where discontent turned into worldwide protests that spread and amplified each other. The crisis of the global capitalist economy and of capitalist society was definitely not the sole cause of the 2011 protests, revolutions and movements, but it was an important context that conditioned these protests. It cannot be an accident that a large number of protests emerged in 2011, a few years after the onset of the crisis. The economic crisis was in many countries articulated with political crises of the state and ideological crises questioning the legitimacy of neoliberalism. The economic crisis is not just a financial crisis because it is an expression of antagonisms of the capitalist economy. It is a crisis of the capitalist economy. Simultaneously due to the connectedness and articulation of the capitalist economy with state power and ideologies, it is a crisis of capitalist society, i.e. the mode of organization of society that is based on the accumulation of money, decision-power/authority and meaning-making power/reputation. The crisis of capitalist society was an important context of the 2011 protests. It was articulated with specific, contextualized factors that varied from country to country and became expressed in specific movements. Such factors included state repression against unions, workers, political movements and citizens, police violence, racism, gender inequality, illiteracy and unequal access to education, cultural imperialism and the cultural ambivalences of modernization, unequal geographies of urban and rural regions, military control of civil society, press and media control, etc.

A crisis of society does not determine the emergence of protests, but it makes them more likely. If and when a specific movement emerges in a particular crisis context and what the goals and political direction of it are, is contingent, undetermined and dependent on complex circumstances. Social movements do not follow algorithms, they are not deterministic, but rather complex, dynamic systems (Fuchs 2006).

The Panic of 1873 that was based on heavy real estate and railroad speculation and that resulted in a worldwide economic crisis known as the Long Depression was followed by a long period of labor unrest, including the riots of the unemployed at New York's Tompkins Square Park in January 1874, the Great US Railroad Strike in 1877, the May 1886 US general strike for the 8 hour working day, the 1892 Homestead steel strike, the 1894 Pullman railway strike and the Pennsylvania Coal Strike of 1902. The Wall Street Crash in 1929 set off the Great Depression, the twentieth century's worst worldwide economic crisis. Political consequences included the French general strikes in 1932 and 1936, the Swiss general strike of 1932, the Nazi Party's (NSDAP) entry into the German Reichstag after the 1930 General Election and its election success in November 1932 that resulted in Hitler's seizure of power in January 1933, the 1933 strike of sailors in the Netherlands, the 1934 Jordaan riot in Amsterdam, the 1934 West Coast Waterfront Strike by sailors in San Francisco, the 1934 Minneapolis strike against trucking companies, the 1934 strike of autoworkers in Toledo, the Jarrow March of unemployed people from North East England to London in 1936, the 1936/1937 Flint Sit-Down Strike by automobile workers at General Motors, the Spanish Civil War 1936-1939, the Second World War 1938-1945.

The 1973 oil and energy crisis resulted in relatively immediate reactions, such as the December 1973 general strike of truck drivers and the UK strike of coalminers and railroad workers in winter 1973/1974, but not in a long period of unrest as in the Long and Great Depressions.

The discussion shows that the amount, intensity and duration of protests following general crises are not determined. It took three years until major protests emerged in 2011 following the 2008 crisis. The first general strike in the USA took place four years after the Long Depression had started in 1873. The French general strike of 1932 and the series of US general strikes in 1934 took place 3 and 5 years after the Great Depression had started. The protest reactions to the oil crisis that started in October 1973 were relatively immediate, but limited in amount, length and intensity. This data shows the unpredictability of the point of time, the intensity, length, contents and results of working class struggles (and social movement struggles in general, including right-wing movements' struggles) that take place in the context of crises.

The Occupy movement is one of the manifestations of protest

movements that have emerged the context of the big crisis. The Occupy Wall Street movement started on September 17th, 2011, when activists occupied Zuccotti Park in New York. The police made them leave the park on November 15th. The two makers of Adbusters Magazine (Kalle Lasn, Micah White) had the idea for the occupation, set up the website occupywallstreet.org and spread the occupation idea to its subscribers via the magazine, a mailing list and a blog. The call text read: "On September 17, we want to see 20,000 people flood into lower Manhattan, set up tents, kitchens, peaceful barricades and occupy Wall Street for a few months. Once there, we shall incessantly repeat one simple demand in a plurality of voices. ... we demand that Barack Obama ordain a Presidential Commission tasked with ending the influence money has over our representatives in Washington. It's time for DEMOCRACY NOT CORPORATOCRACY, we're doomed without it. ... Beginning from one simple demand – a presidential commission to separate money from politics – we start setting the agenda for a new America" (Adbusters 2012). Movements that explicitly used the term "Occupy" also emerged in countries such as Australia, Belgium, Canada, Colombia, Denmark, Finland, France, Germany, Hong Kong, Italy, Malaysia, Mexico, the Netherlands, New Zealand, Nigeria, Norway, Ireland, South Africa, Sweden, Switzerland and the United Kingdom. They were inspired by the Arab Spring revolutions, the Indignant Citizens Movement in Greece and the 15-M Movement in Spain.

In a self-understanding published on the website occupy-wallst.org, Occupy Wall Street describes itself as being the "99% that will no longer tolerate the greed and corruption of the 1%" (http://occupywallst.org/). They positions themselves as class struggle against the 1%: "#ows is fighting back against the corrosive power of major banks and multinational corporations over the democratic process, and the role of Wall Street in creating an economic collapse that has caused the greatest recession in generations. The movement is inspired by popular uprisings in Egypt and Tunisia, and aims to fight back against the richest 1% of people that are writing the rules of an unfair global economy that is foreclosing on our future" (http://occupywallst.org/about/).

The *Declaration of the Occupation of New York City* (http://www.nycga.net/resources/documents/declaration/) speaks out against "corporations, which place profit over people, self-interest over justice, and oppression over equality". In this declaration, the movement says that it is critical of the negative effects of corporations on housing, bailouts, workplace inequality and discrimination, food supply, animal rights, union-ization, higher education, workers' healthcare and wages, privacy protection, freedom of the press, nature, energy supply, medicine, the media, international relations. This shows that the Occupy movement stresses how capitalist interests interact with the social, cultural, political, ecological and technological realms of society and create negative impacts on these realms.

Occupy movements in other countries have formulated comparable goals. Occupy London describes itself as movement "against this injustice and to fight for a sustainable economy that puts people and the environment we live in before corporate profits" (http://occupylondon.org.uk/about). In its Initial Statement passed on October 26th, 2011, Occupy London stressed that the current system is unsustainable, undemocratic and unjust and has negative impacts on citizens, democracy, health services, welfare, education, employment, peace and the planet (http://occupylondon.org.uk/about). Occupy Nigeria describes its goals in the following way: "Let's join together in standing against corruption, poverty, police intimidation, unemployment and inequality of wealth in Nigeria" (https://www.facebook .com/OccupyNigeriaGroup/info). Occupy South Africa argues: "The 1% of people who own and control everything and who are trying to keep the masses enslaved and asleep has to know that we see through their game. We do not have the answers yet – we'll work on it together to restore a fair and humane society flourishing in freedom. All we definitely agree upon is that something is not right" (https://www.facebook.com/occupy sa/info).

The Occupy movement shows the topicality of capitalism, exploitation and class. It has advanced the discussion of a commons-based society as an alternative to capitalism and has made publicly visible the problems of class society.

3. Occupy and Digital Media

David Graeber (2013), who was involved in Occupy Wall Street from the beginning and helped to coin the slogan "We are the 99%", describes the origins and development of Occupy Wall Street. He cites from an email by Micah White (Adbusters), in which the latter wrote that Adbusters understood itself as spreading the idea of the occupation, but not as organizer, for which local people would be needed (Graeber 2013, 35f). Graeber describes that the local organization work started with a meeting of activists that took place on August 2nd, 2011, in Bowling Green Park (Graeber 2013, 23-34). This shows that Adbusters communicated an idea with visual, textual and online media, but that local organizing was a crucial step in bringing about Occupy Wall Street that therefore cannot be considered as a movement that was created online. Graeber explains how working groups were created, among them a communication group that set up an email mailing list and a public relations group. Graeber's account of the organization of Occupy Wall Street illustrates that organizing protests requires face-to-face meetings and contacts of activists. Protests are not created online, but by the social relations of activists that communicate with each other and connect with others. In this process the Occupy activists especially made use of email lists as a communication tool for staying in touch. Live video streaming and Twitter were especially used for reporting from the protest event on September 17th, 2011 (Graeber 2013, 46-54).

An important theoretical question is how to best classify social movements' media use. For doing so, a theory of information is needed. One can distinguish three basic notions of sociality: Durkheim's social facts, Weber's social actions/ relations, Marx and Tönnies' co-operation that can be integrated into a model of human social activity and applied to "social media" (Fuchs 2010b, 2014b). It is based on the assumption that knowledge is a threefold dynamic process of cognition, communication and co-operation (Hofkirchner 2013). Cognition is the necessary prerequisite for communication and the precondition for the emergence of co-operation. Or in other words: in order to co-operate you need to communicate and in order to communicate you need to cognize. Cognition involves the knowledge processes of a single individual. These processes are social in the Durkheimian sense of social facts because the existence of humans in society and therefore social relations shape human knowledge (Fuchs 2010b, 2014b). Humans can only exist by entering social relations with other humans. They exchange symbols in these relations – they communicate. This level corresponds to Weber's notion of social relations. A human being externalizes parts of its knowledge in every social relation. As a result, this knowledge influences others, who change part of their knowledge structures and as response externalize parts of their own knowledge, which results in the differentiation of the first individual's knowledge. A certain number of communications are not just sporadic, but continuous over time and space. In such cases, there is the potential that communication results in co-operation, the shared production of new qualities, new social systems, or new communities with feelings of belonging together. This is the level of co-operative labor and community. It is based on Marx's concept of co-operative labor and Tönnies' notion of community (Fuchs 2010b, 2014b).

Information (cognition), communication and co-operation are three nested and integrated modes of sociality. Every medium can be social in one or more of these senses. All media are information technologies. They provide information to humans. This information enters into the human realm of knowledge as social facts that shape thinking. Information media are, for example: books, newspapers, journals, posters, leaflets, films, television, radio, CDs, DVDs. Some media are also media of communication

– they enable humans' recursive exchange of information in social relations. Examples are letters in love relations, the telegraph and the telephone.

Networked computer technologies enable cognition, communication and co-operation. The classical notion of the medium was confined to the social activities of cognition and communication, whereas the classical notion of technology was confined to the area of labor and production with the help of machines (such as the conveyor belt). The rise of computer technology and computer networks (such as the Internet) has enabled the convergence of media and machines – the computer supports cognition, communication, and co-operative labor (production): it is a classical medium and a classical machine at the same time. Furthermore it has enabled the convergence of production, distribution (communication) and consumption of information – you use only one tool, the networked computer, for these three processes. In contrast to other media (like the press, broadcasting, the telegraph, the telephone), computer networks are not only media of information and communication, but also enable the co-operative production of information. Social movement media can be classified according to the level of information they make use of. This allows distinctions to be made between cognitive, communicative and co-operative cyberprotest (Fuchs 2008, chapter 8.5).

The Occupy movement encompasses all three dimensions of cyberprotest. It makes use of both commercial media (Reddit, Twitter, Facebook, Meetup) as well as alternative, non-commercial, non-profit media (TheGlobalSquare, Occupii, Riseup, Diaspora, N-1). The following table gives an overview classification of online media that Occupy Wall Street and Occupy London link to on their websites.

	Commercial platforms	Non-commercial platforms
Cognition	occupywallstreet-page on the social news service Reddit (http://www.reddit.com/r/occupywallstreet/), Tumblr blog "We are the 99 percent" (http://wearethe99percent.tumblr.com/)	Live video streams (http://occupystreams.org); http://occupywallst.org: blog-based news, protest map, how to occupy guide http://occupylondon.org.uk: blog-based news, live video streams, podcasts (Occupy Radio), newspapers (e.g. Occupied Times, Occupied Wall Street Journal), news services (e.g. Occupy News Network, occupy.com, Occupied Stories), event calendar; live video streams on http://occupii.org/; map-based directory of occupations, map of events, Occupy classifieds, directory of Occupy campaigns on http://www.occupy.net/

Table 8: A classification of the Occupy movement's social media use

Communication	Twitter (e.g. @OccupyWallSt, @OccupyLondon, #OccupyWallstreet, #OWS, #OccupyLSX, #OccupyLondon, #olsx)	Chat (http://occupystreams.org), http://occupywallst.org/: chat and discussion forum (http://occupywallst.org/), Riseup (http://www.riseup.net; chat, email, mailing lists); InterOccupy (http://interoccupy.net), OccupyTalk voice chat (www.occupytalk.org)
Co-operation	Facebook: e.g. Occupy Together (https://www.facebook.com/OccupyWallSt), Occupy London (www.facebook.com/occupylondon), Facebook app Occupy Network, Occupy Together Meetup	SNS Occupii (http://occupii.org/), SNS N-1 (https://n-1.cc), SNS Diaspora* (https://joindiaspora.com/), Occupy wiki (http://wiki.occupy.net) Occupy Pads (http://notes.occupy.net/)

Table 8: Continued.

Occupy Wall Street's website http://occupywallst.org features news in blog format that can be commented on, a collection of live video streams (http://occupystreams.org) from different countries and regions (Occupy Streams) that are each accompanied by a live chat; a map with links to on-going occupations and movement media, social media tools, documents, documentaries and other resources; a how to occupy guide explaining different movement strategies and practices in multiple languages, a discussion forum, a chat, a global map locating on-going occupations, a link to the movement's Twitter account @OccupyWallSt (around 173 000 followers on December 2nd, 2012 and 184 700 on July 1st, 2013) that suggests use of the two hashtags #OccupyWallstreet and #OWS, a link to the page "occupywallstreet" on the social news service reddit, a link to the Facebook page Occupy Together (https://www.face book.com/OccupyWallSt, 416 768 likes on April 25th, 2013, 12:34, BST, 419 213 likes on July 1st, 2013, 16:40 BST).

Occupy London's site http://occupylondon.org.uk includes a link to Occupy London's Twitter account @OccupyLondon (around 36 500 followers on December 2nd, 2012; around 43 000 followers on July 1st, 2013), a link to the Facebook page Occupy the London Stock Exchange (www.facebook.com/occupylondon, around 45 000 likes on December 2nd, 2012; 45 367 likes on July 1st, 2013, 16:42 BST), an event calendar with the possibility to submit new events, the possibility to submit proposals and raise issues for discussion at the General Assembly, a blog with news postings on which one can comment, a directory of registered users who can connect to each other, links to several live video streams, podcasts of Occupy Radio, the Occupied Times, which is a monthly newspaper of the movement that invites contributions to be submitted online, a link to the Occupy News Network, images and videos, a directory of various working groups (such as Website Development, Finance, Economics, Internal Communication, Corporations, Press, The Occupied Times, etc).

There are three dimensions of websites such as Occupy Wall Street and Occupy London and social movements' online media use in general. First, there is *the cognitive dimension* of Occupy's social media use. This includes e.g. online news, blogs, news, images, videos, live video streams, radio streams and podcasts, occupation map, guides, Facebook pages, Reddit news, events calendar and newspaper Occupied Times. InterOccupy (http://interoccupy.net) is a platform, where teleconference calls are scheduled and organised that allows activists to discuss and plan protests actions and campaigns. The Occupy.Network (http://www.occupy.net/) provides a map-based directory of occupations, a map of events, Occupy classifieds, a directory of Occupy campaigns and links to the collaboration tools Occupy Wiki (http://wiki.occupy.net) and Occupy Notes (http://notes.occupy.net/). The cognitive dimension of Occupy media also includes online newspapers (such as the Occupied Times http://theoccupiedtimes.co.uk/ and the Occupied Wall Street Journal) and news services such as the Occupy News Network, Occupied Stories and Occupy.com.

The Occupy News Network (http://occupynewsnetwork .co.uk/) features text-based news, the possibility for online article submission and four live video streams (ONN, OccupyLSX, Global Revolution TV, Timcast) that are partly accompanied by live chats. It describes itself as "repository for information, news and commentary on the global Occupy movement and counter-parts in the worldwide revolution such as the Indignados, Anonymous and the Arab Spring. ... ONN keeps you abreast of developments in the global revolution. Here you can watch livestreams of Occupy protests as they unfold or access archive footage of previous actions. We operate a Criminal Investigations Unit to expose police brutality and abuse of the law; you are invited to upload videos of police brutality and send in your witness statements; our media is our most powerful defence against political repression. We present articles and commentary related to Occupy and the global revolution and we work to hold mainstream media to account by exposing lies and bias" (http://occupynewsnetwork.co.uk/onn/about-us-2/).

Occupied Stories (http://occupiedstories.com) is another Occupy news service. It defines itself as a "story-sharing platform that recognizes the mainstream media's claim to fairness and objectivity as both false and unrealistic – no story is objective, but a point of view. ... Our mission is to encourage critical reflection over blind acceptance and amplify the voices from the front-lines of the occupy movement" (http://occupied-stories.com/about). Also Occupy.com is a news service: It is "a new media channel that will amplify the voices of Occupy. We use media to call for social, economic and environmental justice. We seek to inspire resistance, engagement and the creation of the new world we imagine". It is also "an open invitation to creators of every stripe: journalists, musicians, photographers, painters, filmmakers, poets, game developers, cartoonists, podcasters – every genre, form and style. We're striving to become an open platform, where everyone can post and everyone can curate" (http://www.occupy.com/about/).

Occupy News Network, Occupied Stories and Occupy.com share the characteristics of being citizens media, allowing open submission of content, questioning mainstream media, being partial for the oppressed and having a non-commercial and non-profit character, which are typical characteristics of alternative media (Atton 2002, Fuchs 2010a, Sandoval and Fuchs 2010). Second, there is *the communicative dimension* of cyberprotest in the context of Occupy. It features, for example, blog comments, discussion forum, chats, Twitter profile and hashtags, Facebook pages and Reddit news comments. Riseup (http://www.rise up.net) "provides online communication tools for people and groups working on liberatory social change" (chat, email, mailing lists). The project is funded by donations. The communication is encrypted and does not store IP addresses because Riseup

opposes "the rise of a surveillance society" (https://help
.riseup.net/de/security) and thinks "it is vital that essential
communication infrastructure be controlled by movement
organizations and not corporations or the government"
(https://help.riseup.net/de/about-us). It is a project that wants to
"aid in the creation of a free society, a world with freedom from
want and freedom of expression, a world without oppression or
hierarchy, where power is shared equally" by "providing
communication and computer resources to allies engaged in
struggles against capitalism and other forms of oppression"
(https://help.riseup.net/de/about-us).

OccupyTalk (www.occupytalk.org) uses the open source
voice communication software Mumble in order to enable voice
chat of Occupy activists for organizational purposes. Third, there
is *the collaborative/co-operative dimension* of Occupy's cyberprotest.
Co-operation is comprised of collaborative work (Marx) and
community (Tönnies). These two dimensions are represented in
the Occupy movement by wikis (collaborative work) and social
networking sites (community).

Tumblr is a commercial photo blog platform. The Tumblr blog
"We are the 99 percent" (http://wearethe99percent.tumblr.com/)
is a group blog that features images of Occupy movements,
where members or participants show self-written signs that
explain the story of why they are part of the 99%. "Let us know
who you are. Take a picture of yourself holding a sign that
describes your situation - for example, 'I am a student with
$25,000 in debt,' or 'I needed surgery and my first thought wasn't
if I was going to be okay, it was how I'd afford it.' Below that,
write 'I am the 99 percent.' Below that, write 'occupywallst.org'"
(http://wearethe99percent.tumblr.com/submit).

http://wiki.occupy.net is a collaboratively edited wiki that
presents information about events, projects, campaigns and
knowledge related to the Occupy movement. Everyone can edit
it.

Occupy Together Meetup (http://www.meetup.com/occupyto-gether/) is a domain on the Meetup platform that allows activists to schedule and join local Occupy meetings. The Facebook app Occupy Network (http://www.occupynetwork.com/) is "designed to help connect all the local organizing happening on facebook into something bigger". It displays Facebook pages, groups, users, discussions, as well as tweets related to the Occupy movement. It represents the commercial community dimension of Occupy's social media use. But there are also non-commercial platforms associated with Occupy.

The Global Square (http://theglobalsquare.org/) is a non-commercial non-profit social networking site funded by donations. It "respects privacy for individuals and transparency for public organizations and actions. As a social environment we will facilitate open communication while retaining individual control over privacy. We support the right of individuals to assemble, associate and collaborate and to choose the manner of doing so". "The goal of the Global Square is to perpetuate and spread the creative and cooperative spirit of the occupations and transform this into lasting forms of social organization, at the global as well as the local level". Facebook and Twitter are perceived as being too limited for the Occupy movement: "Facebook and Twitter have been very helpful for disseminating basic information and aiding mass mobilization, they do not provide us with the tools for extending our participatory model of decision-making beyond the direct reach of the assemblies and up to the global level. Neither do they provide us with project management tools for our working groups". The site sees itself as complimentary tool to meetings that involve physical presence: "The aim of the platform, in this respect, should not be to replace the physical assemblies but rather to empower them by providing the online tools for local and (trans)national organization and collaboration". One basic goal is "news without censorship" by the government.

Occupii (http://occupii.org/) is a non-commercial non-profit social networking site and live video streaming platform funded by donations that is associated with the Occupy movement. On April 28th, 2013 (17:55, BST) it had 5642 members. The project is built on the belief that mainstream media manipulate and censor the public sphere: "One person in isolation cannot hope to stand against the behemoths that are the 'Mainstream Media'. But together we can enable those willing and able to be the eyes and ears of the online communities to do so. ... We are already seeing crackdowns on protestors through various means including usage of draconian legislation brought in specifically to create a police state during this year. *We know mainstream media is corrupted.* This will be even more prevalent during 2012. We cannot rely on MSM for any sort of reliable, unbiased reportage. ... We wish to put together a dedicated livestreaming team comprised of 2 elements: one 'on the ground' team of 4 people with 3 independent livestreaming backpacks, allowing us to bring you footage from many events and many angles of same events, creating the link between the events and the online communities. The other element is an 'online' team of producers, editors, graphic designers, writers and 'support' team for the 'ground' crew. ... The total cost of the 3 backpacks is about £1700 ($2740)" (http://occupii.org/page/donate). The terms of service are relatively short (978 words on April 28th, 2013) and do not contain any clauses about data use for advertising.

The overview presented in this chapter shows that the Occupy movement makes use of a variety of online platforms. The task the OccupyMedia! Survey was to obtain data about activists' assessments of social media and their usage practices.

4. Research Method: The OccuyMedia! Survey

In planning research, it is important to clarify which strategy is to be used for collecting data, from whom data is collected and how this is achieved (Punch 2005, 63). In order to give answers to the research questions, a questionnaire was designed. It was the foundation for the implementation of an online survey.

Earl Babbie (2010, chapter 4) argues that there are steps in the design and conduction of a research project: conceptualization, choice of a method, operationalization, population and sampling, observation, data processing, analysis and application. Alan Bryman (2012, chapter 1) distinguishes the following steps: literature review, conceptualization and theory foundations, formulation of research questions, sampling, data collection, data analysis, write-up.

Literature review, conceptualization and theory foundations can be combined into a first step called *the conceptual phase*. Choice of a method and formulation of research questions are part of the conceptual phase because one needs to know which questions to ask in order to identify the central concepts and theoretical approached needed for undertaking an analysis. *Operationalization* is the phase that connects concepts and theory to empirical research. *Sampling, data collection* and *data analysis* are three quite distinct phases identified by both Babbie and Bryman. Babbie distinguishes between data observation and processing, which can be combined because observation requires recording, storing or organizing data. Also the analysis phase is a form of data processing, so processing data cannot be clearly separated from data collection and analysis, but is rather part of both. Write-up and application can be combined into one stage, forming the *interpretation phase*.

The *conceptualization* of the research presented in this work came out of an engagement with the question of what roles social media play in contemporary revolutions and rebellions. Blogger Andrew Sullivan (2009) wrote about the 2009 Iranian protests that "the revolution will be twittered", which contributed to the widespread myth of Twitter revolutions. After the UK riots, the media and politicians claimed that Blackberry phones and social media orchestrated the riots (see Fuchs 2012a). Social media scholars who presented social media as radically new and as radically changing politics positively reflected the general overemphasis of the implications of social media for politics in their writings. Clay Shirky argued that the political use of "social media" ultimately enhances freedom (see: Gladwell and Shirky 2010).

In response to the techno-euphoria about social media, Malcolm Gladwell (2010) argued that activists in revolutions and rebellions risk their lives and risk becoming victims of violence conducted by the police or the people their protest is directed at. Taking the courage to face these dangers would require strong social ties and friendships with others in the movement. Activism would involve high risks. Evgeny Morozov (2009) concurs with Gladwell's argument of slacktivism as "feel-good online activism that has zero political or social impact. It gives those who participate in 'slacktivist' campaigns an illusion of having a meaningful impact on the world without demanding anything more than joining a Facebook group". Morozov (2010) also argues that the notion of "Twitter revolution" is based on a belief in cyber-utopianism – "a naive belief in the emancipatory nature of online communication that rests on a stubborn refusal to acknowledge its downside" (Morozov 2010, xiii) that combined with Internet-centrism forms a techno-deterministic ideology. Morozov stresses that information technologies are also used as tools for the surveillance of activists and are often owned and sold by Western companies for such purposes.

During 2011, the year of the revolutions in Tunisia and Egypt and other uprisings, there was an echo in the mass media, politics and scholarship that resembled the earlier talk about Twitter and Facebook revolutions. So for example Wael Ghonim (2012), the administrator of the Facebook page "We are all Khaled Said", argued that the Egyptian revolution was a "revolution 2.0" facilitated by Facebook and Twitter. For Evgeny Morozov (2013, 127), Ghonim is "a man who lives and breathes Internet-centrism" – an ideology that reduces societal change to the Internet.

Manuel Castells (2012) argued in his book *Networks of Outrage and Hope* that the Tunisian and Egyptian revolutions as well as the protests in Iceland, the Spanish 15-M movement and the Occupy Wall Street movement were born and based upon, as well as diffused and maintained by, the Internet. In a review essay of this book (Fuchs 2012b), I argued that Castells mirrors the techno-determinism that can so frequently be found in the mass media, politics and populist scholarship and neither provides a theoretical nor an empirical understanding of the role of social media and the Internet in contemporary political movements.

W. Lance Bennett and Alexandra Segerberg (2012, 2013) argue that Occupy and many other contemporary protest movements are based on the logic of connective action, in which there is no or little hierarchy and organization coordination, social media take "the role of established political organizations" (Bennett and Segerberg 2012, 742) and are realms through which "easily personalized ideas" (e.g. "We are the 99%"), which the authors term personal action frames, are shared and spread. Bennett and Segerberg oppose the logic of connective action to the logic of collective action and thereby over-stress individualization and separation. But do protest movement not necessarily have specific collective features? This thought becomes evident if one thinks about Occupy Wall Street's occupation of a common space and its collective demands for "direct and transparent participatory democracy", "personal and collective responsibility", empowerment, education as human right, open technology, culture and knowledge.[1] Collective goals, values and identities are the outcome of discussion and communication processes in social movements. Bennett and Segerberg's approach creates the impression that Occupy has no collective identities, goals and values at all and is a pure combination of individualized politics. They also neglect how contemporary social movements are facing the collective power of institutions such as the state, the police, corporations, banks, tabloid media, etc. Mimicking Margaret Thatcher's slogan "there is no such thing as society"[2], they are convinced that in Occupy and comparable movements there is no such things as collectivity. Occupy is a movement that aims at reclaiming the commons of society. It is therefore a movement for making privatized and privately controlled resources collectively available to all. Occupy's networked action has a collective dimension – the common coming-together in public space through which collective values, demands and goals are formed in order to reclaim and strengthen the commons. It is in this sense that Jodi Dean (2012), in contrast to individualistic interpretations, argues that Occupy is a movement oriented on the commons.

In his book *Tweets and the Streets. Social Media and Contemporary Activism*, Paolo Gerbaudo (2012) challenges on theoretical and empirical grounds the assumptions of Castells, Bennett/Segerberg and others that the Internet brings about leaderless movements. He interviewed 80 activists in the USA, Egypt, Spain, the United Kingdom, Tunisia and Greece about their use of social media in protests and found that although contemporary social movements claim that they are leaderless networks, there are soft leaders who make use of social media for choreographing protests and "constructing a *choreography of assembly*" (Gerbaudo 2012, 139). Considering the Arab Spring, Miriyam Aouragh (2012, 529) argues that the "overt fascination with social media gave the impression that the revolutions were mainly middle class and secular. Western experiences were taken as the model" or the Arab revolutions were "evaluated through the lens of modernity", based on the assumption that "social media plays an important role in developing a sense of modernity". Overcoming short-circuited analyses of social media's role in revolutions would require a dialectical and historical Marxist analysis. Aouragh shares Gerbaudo's analysis and connects it to a Marxist theory framework.

Understanding the role of social media in political movements requires complex theoretical models and empirical research that gets at how relevant these media have been in their protest experiences. My own contribution to this critical project at the conceptual level has been a criticism of approaches such as the one by Castells which I consider overtly reductionist, as well as theoretical work on social movements, social media in the crisis conjuncture of contemporary capitalism (Fuchs 2012a, b, 2014a, b).

In order to also contribute something at the level of empirical research, in autumn 2012 I came up with the idea of conducting the OccupyMedia! Survey. The aim of this project is to analyse Occupy activists' assessment of the role of social media in their movement, their actual usage of these and other media for obtaining and publishing news, protest communication and mobilization as well as their assessment of the relationship between commercial and non-commercial social media.

The survey was based on the following research questions:

1. How do activists define the Occupy movement? What kind of movement is it for them? (see the results and analysis in sections 5.2 and 6.1)
2. What is activists' perceived role of social media in the Occupy movement (see the results and analysis in sections 5.3 and 6.2)?
3. How often do Occupy activists use certain media and communication forms? (see the results and analysis in

sections 5.4 and 6.3)

3.1. How often do Occupy activists use certain media and communication forms for informing themselves about protests and occupations?

3.2. How often do Occupy activists create content for or about the movement with the help of certain media?

3.3. How often do Occupy activists use certain media and communication forms for communication with other activists?

3.4. How often do Occupy activists use certain media and communication forms for trying to mobilize people for protests and occupations?

4. Which advantages and disadvantages do Occupy activists see in relation to the movement's use of commercial digital media and alternative, non-commercial, non-profit digital media? (see the results and analysis in sections 5.5 and 6.4)

The *operationalization* phase focused on constructing a question-naire for a quantitative and qualitative online survey. Studying how activists assess the role of social media in their protests requires that they can give qualitative feedback. Quantitative research is also needed for evaluating the degree of relevance and obtaining an understanding of what role social media play in contemporary movements. The constructed questionnaire consisted of four single choice questions, 1 multiple-choice question, 16 open-ended questions, 1 binary question and 86 interval scaled questions. The survey was directed at Occupy activists as potential respondents and was implemented with the help of the online survey tool SurveyMonkey. Using an online survey tool allows reaching a larger number of respondents in a faster time, has a rather low resource-intensity, automatically generates a data file for analysis and allows logical branching in the questionnaire (Babbie 2010, 283–287). A potential negative aspect is that an online survey is limited to Internet users (Babbie 2010, 284). The Occupy General Survey (http://www.occupyresearch.net/category/survey/) shows that Occupy activists tend to be heavy Internet users, which shows that it is a group that can be ideally reached online. On the first screen of the survey, users were informed about the purely academic purpose of the study, that data is treated in an anonymous and confidential way (Punch 2005, 100) and that they give informed consent to the storage, analysis of the obtained data and publication of the results. The questionnaire was online from November 6th, 2012, until February 20th, 2013.

A pre-test was conducted. An invitation to participate in it was sent to 13 users. 10 of them completed the survey and provided feedback. As a result, the following changes were undertaken:

- 4 sets of questions were turned from drop-down boxes into matrices in order to improve user-friendliness.
- The length of 6 text fields was increased from one line to three lines in order to invite longer comments.
- The language of buttons was changed from German to English.
- Standardisation of interval length in answers to frequency questions.
- Splitting of long matrix questions into two matrices for each.

The next stage was to define the *sampling* strategy. Resource limits did not allow translating the questionnaire into other languages and analysing non-English data. It is difficult to draw a boundary between who is an Occupy activist and who is not. The only meaningful way of operationalizing membership is to say that any person involved in contemporary protests who defines her-/himself as Occupy activists is an Occupy activist. The Occupy Wall Street Movement popularized the label

"Occupy". Movements that have adopted the label in their name tend to perceive themselves as being connected to Occupy Wall Street and to share its overall goals. We therefore did not restrict potential survey respondents to Occupy activists in New York or the USA, but allowed responses by anybody who was actively protesting and identified him-/herself as Occupy activist. Given that the survey was conducted in English, it was clear that it will mainly attract respondents in countries, where English is a first language. Given that there are also activists in other countries who understand themselves as Occupy activists and that Occupy movements in different countries tend to share overall goals such as the criticism of neoliberalism, the 1% and austerity measures, and all tend to have experiences in occupying public spaces, a significant degree of comparable experiences that transgresses national boundaries seems to be given. Respondents from countries, where English is not the first language, were therefore admitted to the survey and included in the analysis. At the same time it was clear that it would be likely that we mainly reach out to activists in countries, where English is the first language, and that respondents from this background would therefore dominate the sample. Limited resources did not allow conducting the survey in multiple languages, although conducting the same survey in different contexts in non-English languages is an important project that hopefully somebody will be able to undertake in the future.

We did not include respondents, who are sympathizers of the movement, but have not participated in protests. It would be interesting to study the opinions of these people in a separate survey, but they cannot provide meaningful information about the role of online media in street protests. The first question in the survey was therefore a binary filter question, asking: "Have you ever participated in any activities of the Occupy movement?" The survey ended for those, who answered "No" to this question. Out of 857 responses to the first question, there were 377 (44.0%) "no" and 480 (56.0%) "yes" answers. Because of limited resources for the analysis, it was necessary to limit the survey to a certain number of respondents (Punch 2005, 101). The basic cut-off point was a maximum of 500 respondents, who answered the filter question with "yes". The actual cut-off taken was at 480 respondents. Given that the survey was conducted online, activists who are not Internet users were automatically excluded from participation. But given that the aim of the project was to analyse the social media use of Occupy activists, the target groups were not all Occupy activists, but only those who employ such online platforms.

A random sampling strategy of respondents is best for achieving a sample that is representative of the population (Babbie 2010, 198; Punch 2005, 102). The conducted survey therefore used probability sampling based on random selection. Random sampling was achieved in two ways: On the one hand, we regularly posted invitations to participate on Internet platforms that are frequented by Occupy activists. On the other hand, we regularly visited online chat forums and social media groups used by the Occupy movement, where we selected users by systematic sampling (every second user, see Babbie 2010, 211-214) and sent them survey invitations. If there was no direct contact possibility for a user, then the next available one was chosen instead.

Data collection was the next step in the research process. The director of this study (Christian Fuchs) and two research assistants (Susann Krieglsteiner, Taghrid Baba) invited potential respondents to participate and promoted the survey in the Occupy movement. The basic principle was to not limit the spread of invitations to one online medium, but to use multiple channels. The basic principle was to reach out to Occupy activists who use social media via the online channels that they use.

We tried to find potential respondents by informing and communicating regularly with users who are likely to be Occupy activists on online spaces in the following ways:

- *Blogs*: We conducted a search for bloggers who are associated with the Occupy movement. This resulted in a list of around 60 people. We contacted them and asked them if they can participate in the survey and pass the invitation on to people in their Occupy contact networks.
- *Mailing lists*: We posted survey invitations to mailing lists of the Occupy movement: Occupy London, RiseUp: Occupy mailing lists, N-1 mailing lists (Take the Square International, 15-M-News, Acapadasol), Occupy.net mailing lists (National, NYC-tech-discuss, OWSContent, S17, S17-discussion, tech-discuss)
- *Online news articles*: We published the news article "Why social media research matters for Occupy" on the Occupy News Network (http://occupynewsnetwork.co.uk/why-social-media-research-matters-for-occupy/). It contained a link to the survey and an invitation to participate.
- *Social networking sites*: We posted survey invitations on the walls of the Facebook pages of Occupy Wall Street (2 pages), Occupy Together and Occupy London (2 pages). We created a Facebook page that advertised the survey and provided a link to it. The page was updated regularly with information about media use in the Occupy movement. We sent invitations to participate to users on the social networking site occupii.org.
- *Twitter*: We posted survey invitations on Twitter by employing hashtags that are used by the Occupy movement: #1world1struggle, #25mgr, #28ogr, #60WallSt, #acampadaberlin, #acampadaparis, #agoraroma, #echtedemokratie, #europeanrevolution, #frenchrevolution, #globalchange, #greekrevolution, #indignati, #indignes, #italianrevolution, #LibertySquare, #marchabruselas, #marcheparis2012, #marchtoathens,

#NoRTWMI, #n17, #occupy, #occupyamsterdam, #occupy-belgium, #occupyboston, #occupybrussels, #occupyevery-thing, #occupyfrance, #occupygent, #occupyitaly, #occupyla, #occupyliege, #occupylondon, #occupylsx, #occupynl, #occupyoakland, #occupyoregon, #occupysf, #occupytoronto, #occupywallstreet, #ows, #rbnews, #saveMI, #skg, #syntagma, #takethesquare, #takewallstreet, #usdor, #walkupy, #wealloccupy.

- *Video streams:* We posted survey invitations in the chats of Occupy channels on live video streams: Global Revolution TV, occupystreams.org, Occupydata.
- *Websites*: We contacted administrators of websites that are related to the movement and asked them to post an invitation to participate in the survey: Adbusters magazine, Democracy Now!, D.C. Mic Check, IndigNACIÓN, Interoccupy News, Michael Moore's website, Occupy.com, Occupy.net, Occupy Boston, Occupied Chicago Tribune, Occupy Delaware, Occupy Directory, Occupy France, Occupy News Network, Occupy Los Angeles, Occupy London, Occupy Miami, Occupy Montreal, Occupy Oakland, Occupy Philly, Occupy Portland, Occupy Prisoners, Occupy San Francisco, Occupy Seattle, Occupy Sydney, Occupy Together, Occupy Union Square, Occupy Wall Street, Occupied Stories, Occupied Times of London, Occupied Wall Street Journal, Portland Occupier, Occupy Philly Media, Occupy Seattle, Occupy Sydney, Occupy the Farm, Occupy the RNC, Occupied Stories, Occupy Writers, People Not Profit, Searching for Occupy, Take the Square, Tidal, WBAI Radio website, Women Occupy.

Data analysis was conducted with the help of SPSS Statistics Version 20. SurveyMonkey allows downloading an SPSS dataset. Some variables that should have numeric values due to the standard settings of the survey software automatically contained text strings, which required some recoding work. 377 entries of respondents, who indicated that they were not Occupy activists in their answers to the filter questions, were deleted from the dataset. There were 51 respondents who indicated that they participated in the Occupy movement, but left the survey before answering the next question. We also deleted these respondents from the dataset. The result was a dataset with N=429 respondents that was used for the analysis. The outcomes of the data analysis are presented in Section 5. Section 6 provides an interpretation of the data.

5. Results of the OccupyMedia! Survey

5.1. Analysis of the Respondents' Demographic Data

Country	Frequency	Percent	Valid Percent
UK	56	13.1	13.4
USA	236	55.0	56.5
Australia	18	4.2	4.3
Azerbaijan	1	.2	.2
Bahamas	1	.2	.2
Bahrain	1	.2	.2
Belgium	4	.9	1.0
Brazil	1	.2	.2
Canada	38	8.9	9.1
Finland	1	.2	.2
France	2	.5	.5
Germany	9	2.1	2.2
Greece	4	.9	1.0
India	1	.2	.2
Ireland	3	.7	.7
Italy	1	.2	.2
Netherlands	14	3.3	3.3
New Zealand	1	.2	.2
Poland	1	.2	.2
Portugal	1	.2	.2
Romania	1	.2	.2
Slovenia	1	.2	.2
Spain	13	3.0	3.1
Sweden	7	1.6	1.7
Switzerland	1	.2	.2
Taiwan	1	.2	.2
Total	418	97.4	100.0
Missing responses	11	2.6	

Table 9: Countries, in which the OccupyMedia! Survey's respondents predominantly participated in protests

Table 9 shows the countries the respondents were coming from.

It indicates that 55.0% of the respondents were from the USA, 13.1% from the UK, 9.1% from Canada and 4.2% from Australia. This means that a total of 81.4% of the respondents were from these four English-speaking countries. This result can be explained by the circumstance that the survey invitations were predominantly distributed on English websites and that respondents prefer to conduct surveys in their mother tongue. Resource limitations did not allow translation of the questionnaire into other languages.

We asked the respondents how they assessed their political standpoint on a scale, where 1 means left-wing and 10 right-wing. 60.2% considered themselves to be fairly left wing (sum of the percentage shares for 1 and 2), only 1.7% fairly right wing (sum of the percentage shares for 9 and 10). The median was 2.0 and the mean value 2.5 (standard deviation: 1.8). The data shows that the OccupyMedia! respondents were fairly left wing. Given that the general topic of the Occupy movement is the critique of inequality and the power of capital, this result is feasible and is likely to signify a general characteristic of the overall Occupy movement.

N=415	1=left	2	3	4	5
Frequency	164	86	77	24	49
Percent	39.5%	20.7%	18.6%	5.8%	11.8%
	6	7	8	9	10=right
Frequency	5	2	1	0	7
Percent	1.2%	0.5%	0.2%	0%	1.7%

Table 10: OccupyMedia! Survey respondent's self-assessment of their political worldview

The survey contained questions that asked activists about the intensity of their participation in certain protest activities during a month in which they were active in the Occupy movement. I combined five of these variables in the following way in order to calculate an index that measures the intensity of a respondent's protest activities. Details of how the protest intensity index was calculated are shown in Table 11. The protest intensity index measures the intensity of protest activities such as marching, occupying, or organizing protests. A value of 0 means that the respondent never participated in any protest activities of the Occupy movement, whereas 24 means that the respondent very frequently participated in such activities, namely at least 60 times.

Thinking about the Occupy movement, how often have you participated in any of the following activities:	
A: Marched in a protest	1=Never
B: Visited an Occupy camp	2=1-3 times
	3=4-6 times
C: Stayed over night in an Occupy camp	4=7-9 times
	5=More often
D: Participated in a General Assembly	Protest intensity index = $A + B + C + D + E + F - 6$
E: Spoke or expressed an opinion in an Occupy General Assembly	Possible values = $\{0,1,...24\}$ 0...very low protest participation 24...very high protest participation
F: Organized a protest event	

Table 11: Calculation of the protest intensity index

Babbie (2010, 165ff) explains that in constructing a composite index one must make sure that the included variables measure the same phenomenon. Calculating all bivariate relations between the variables can test this. "You should probably drop any item that is not related to several other items" (Babbie 2010, 166). All six variables included in the protest intensity index were correlated. All correlations were significant at the 0.01-level and ranged between 0.444 and 0.863. This is an indication that the variables measure the same phenomenon and are suited for combination in a composite index. Missing data can impact the quality of a composite index negatively (Babbie 2010, 172). In our dataset, all included respondents answered all six questions that were asked in order to assess the frequency of protest activities. 57.6% of the activists had a protest intensity index between 0 and 12, meaning that they had a low or medium intensity of protest activities, 42.4% had a value of more than 12. 24.8% had a value of 19 or above, meaning that around one quarter of the respondents were heavy activists.

In the presentation of qualitative results that follows only example quotations for specific trends are provided. More examples can be found by viewing the full dataset.

5.2. Defining the Occupy Movement

We wanted to find out how Occupy activists defined their movement. Therefore one question in the OccupyMedia! Survey was: "Can you please define what the Occupy movement is for you? Try to think about the movement's activists, adversaries, goals, strategies, political worldviews and its context in society. For me, the Occupy movement is … (please complete)".

A social movement is a reaction to certain problems in society. It has specific causal explanations of these problems and therefore identifies opponents and causes of these problems. Its struggles are directed against these opponents and aim at the solution of the identified problems. Therefore a social movement also has specific political goals. In the struggles for achieving these goals, it uses specific protest methods. A social movement is a form of collective political action. In order to act, it needs internal organization structures. This means that opponents and problems, political goals, protest methods and organizational structures are four important aspects of a social movement. We conducted a topical coding of the answers by creating four variables, one each for opponents/problems, goals, methods and organizational structures. In the coding process, we identified for each answer the topics that respondents identified with the Occupy movement. The task was not to quantify how important our respondents considered certain topics and themes to be for the Occupy movement, but rather to create an overview of which issues are relevant for the movement.

5.2.1. Societal Problems and the Occupy Movement's Opponents

Capitalism

A major topic mentioned by the respondents was that capitalism causes problems and that Occupy opposes capitalism. They said that Occupy "oppose[s] the capitalist status quo" (#8) and is a "gathering of people who know that the current system of capitalism is unsustainable" (#10). Other typical answers were, for example:

- Occupy's goal is to "abolish wage-slavery & thereby establish a global society without possession, money, commerce, countries or religion as John Lennon imagined ... It is Capital which is capitalist, in the words of Karl Marx. Hence OCCUPYING CAPITAL i.e. all means of production & socialization will be the last ditched fight to reach the goal" (#15)
- Occupy is "a deconstruction of economic inequality and exploitation across the globe and within our communities" (#69).
- "Occupy is about drawing attention to the excesses of mature capitalism. How our societies are controlled

increasingly by fewer and fewer people. In particular, those with accumulated extreme wealth and those in top positions of power in mega-corporations, and how their ever increasing wealth and power, is eroding our democracies so that ordinary citizens / voters have less and less real power at ballot box as more and more decisions are strongly influenced / dictated by / and made affecting our lives by unelected powerful people using their power to affect decisions by elected people ... as well as directly in the market environments in which they operate. In summary... Power corrupts ... and this is increasingly a greater problem as money and power always go together ... and the money / wealth is being concentrated in fewer and fewer hands with less and less opportunity in a mature capitalist market for mobility of power" (#79).

- "It is a defense in the class war being waged by the super wealthy and their ... political parties" (#86).
- "Occupy is an anarchist movement dedicated to abolishing capitalism and the state" (#105)
- "Money has become a god, an end in itself. This is destructive" (#130).
- Occupy is "redefining the class war" (#206).
- "We live in an international monetary war against humanity" (#207).
- Occupy is "popular democratic resistance to the injustices of Capitalism" (#222).
- "Anti-capitalist. It is the only term that can be used to describe what OWS is about. The issue for OWS is simple. The majority of people, in a general sense, know capitalism is a bullshit economic theology that does not benefit the vast majority of the people, but what will replace it is not clear. This is why occupy has never had a set of demands. We have to cure the cancer before we can recommend a recover program" (#260).

- "A means for activists to get together and fight against the evils of capitalism and to form a socialist revolution" (#274).
- Occupy is "opposing the fascist tyranny of corporate greed" (#346)
- Occupy is "a group of people protesting against a exploitative and wrong system" (#394)   The respondents did not consider capitalism as an isolated topic, but saw it as being connected to other issues, such as corruption and racism. One respondent defined Occupy as "a movement that brings awareness to the general public about the greed of corporations and the corruption of our political system because of that greed. ... It is all about the inequities that have been created through greed and corruption of a very small percentage of the world's population. It has raised awareness about racism and class warfare. It shows the effect of corporate rule on our minds, our bodies, our relationships, the environment, the government – on all aspects of our lives" (#56).

The basic argument that the activist makes is that the logic of capital accumulation that is characteristic for corporations also shapes politics and everyday life so that people use others like an instrument. The result is corruption and racism.

Injustice, inequality and unfairness

A topic closely related to capitalism is that the respondents feel that this system is unjust and unfair and results in inequality. They stress the unfairness of wealth gaps between the rich and the poor; between well-off managers and shareholders on the one hand and regular employees as well as the unemployed, the homeless and precarious workers on the other.

Occupy would be "the awakening to global injustice" (#212), "a much needed visceral eruption of frustration towards the overwhelming inequities in modern society" (#247), "a broad coalition of people concerned about the social and economic injustice of late capitalism" (#393), "a direct decentralized attack on a system of capitalism that makes life miserable for millions and the governance that makes it possible" (#257) and a "protest against the fact that there's lots of poverty and unemployment while bankers created the crises and that governments support them, while we the 99% are paying for this" (#338).

Respondents stressed "the unfair salary distribution of wealth" (#245), that it is "a right to express and protest inequalities in our government such as discrimination, racism and sexism, wars, violence against women and children, fraud by banks, religious extremism, gun control, I can go on" (#282). "Homelessness and poverty in New York are widespread, deep phenomena that the city tries it's best to hide, and Occupy brought it to light in the opulent heart of the financial system" (#28).

Austerity measures

The respondents not only feel that as a result of capitalist exploitation wealth distribution is highly unequal in the world, they also think that the wrong people are paying a high price for the crisis. Neoliberalism, the regime of flexible accumulation and finance capitalism resulted in the relative lowering of wages and high growth of profits. These profits were to a large degree invested in high-risk financial instruments. More and more wage earners could, due to the relative lowering of their salaries, no longer afford to pay for basic needs such as housing and consumption goods and therefore went into debt and mortgaged their houses.

The whole situation resulted in many countries in a highly volatile economy, consumer indebtedness and low purchasing power, which fuelled the crisis. As a reaction to the crisis, many governments bailed out banks with taxpayers' money worth billion of dollars and later announced budget cuts, tax increases and austerity measures that hit the working population hard. This means that the working class was first expropriated by neoliberal class struggle that decreased wages in order to increase profits and was then expropriated another time by cuts in state benefits, welfare and having to pay more taxes for fewer state services.

The austerity measures are an important topic for the Occupy movement: Occupy is a "people's movement born from the acknowledgement that the wrong people are paying for the crisis" (#108). "We refuse to pay for the banks' crisis. We do not accept the cuts as either necessary or inevitable" (#109). "They shine a light on the Austerity Agenda that is being enacted by every Western Government and to try and organized a people led response to the Agenda" (#367).

Corruption

The respondents see corruption as an important topic of Occupy. They consider it to be not simply a phenomenon, where governments abuse power, but also see it as a feature of the financial system. They say that one of Occupy's goals is the "control of corrupt governments in power" (#30), that it is "a reaction to international financial corruption" (#63) and "a desperate attempt to raise mass awareness of the corruption of the current global political, monetary and military systems" (#71). Occupy would be a "movement that gives attention to the abuses in the financial sector" (#155) and "an international people's movement opposing the tyranny of the corporate financial sector, and advocating for/living out horizontal direct democracy and mutual aid" (#203).

Police state, the centralization of political power, war, violence, racism and homophobia

Other concerns that were less frequently mentioned were the

emergence of a police state, the centralization of political power, war, violence, racism and homophobia: Occupy is a "movement that had the potential to create alternatives to the US police state" (#35). It opposes the "centralisation of power in political and banking elites who are not democratic and open in their dealing and which badly effect the environment and the 99%" (#46). One goal would be to protect "our human rights and the U.S. constitution to make this a better world and to turn weapons into plowshares to end all wars and create organized love amongst one another" (#137). "It is a movement against systems of violence" (#239), "a movement of the 99%, that is, a movement against an economic system that produces and requires widening economic inequality, which is also fundamentally racist and homophobic" (#263).

5.2.2. Goals
Social movements not only have opponents and not only protest against certain problems and forms of stratification in society, but they also set themselves certain political goals that they struggle for.

Alternatives to capitalism
A certain share of respondents say that the goal is to establish alternatives to capitalism:

- Occupy's goal is "an alternative political-economic order to capitalism" (#11).
- "Occupy is a movement for an economic system that puts people before profit" (#263).
- Occupy "is the construction of an alternative to capitalism" (#352).
- Occupy has "a chance to end the horror of capitalism" (#357).
- Occupy is "a step towards overthrowing capitalism"

(#380).

- "It's a movement for a fairer world, for rights for everyone and against capitalism. It's remarkable that so many people were willing to get arrested ... We are the 99%" (#394).
- "To abolish capitalism forever and any system similar to it in any way" (#420).

Participatory democracy

Another important goal mentioned is the establishment of a new form of democracy, a participatory democracy, in which the people are in control of politics, the economy and everyday life:

- Occupy is "a forum to empower people to participate, shape and determine the society we live in" (#9).
- Occupy has "the feeling that there needs to be a grass-roots alternative to the top-down mess we are in" (#41).
- This goal includes the desire for a people-controlled economy: "The only way to win back control of society from the corporations to the people" (#65).
- "Our ideal for the future society is a democracy from the ground up based on the ideals of mutual aid and solidarity" (#105).
- Occupy is "a way to prepare ourselves to a more distributed society in a peer-2-peer economy (the development of small-scale productivity)" (#186).
- Occupy is "people power" (#208).
- Occupy means "reclaiming democracy over corporatocracy" (#400).

Connected to the idea of participatory democracy is the movement's view that the 99% should take back the control of the world from the 1% who are in control now:

- "WE ARE 99% AND WE CAN DO IT!" (#207).

- Occupy is "a movement of the 99%" (#263).
- "A global collective vs the stratified plutocratic elite and the injustices they seek to bear down upon us the 99% in order to increase their wealth and power and influence (the 1%)" (#284).
- "For me the Occupy movement is the 99% trying to stop their repression at the hands of the 1% and campaign for social justice" (#306).
- Occupy is "the 99% of the population standing up against the forced control from the 1%" (#308).

A just, fair and equitable society

Respondents in the OccupyMedia! survey argue that a just, fair and equitable society is an important goal:

- Occupy struggles for "global social and economic justice" (#1).
- Occupy's goal is "more equitable treatment for all of the people, worldwide" (#45).
- Occupy is "about fairness in all its forms. Fair stewardship of the planet for the next generations. Fairness in democracy in reducing plutocracy and increasing the voice of the ordinary people. Fairness in reducing the wealth gap between the 1 and the 99%" (#61).
- Occupy is "the struggle for justice for the 99% and the pursuit of a better world" (#84).
- "Occupy has changed the conversation and allowed some footing for those who want social and economic justice" (#89).
- "We want structural change towards authentic global equality" (#109).
- "An attempt to flatten the social structure. For instance: the adoption of a more progressive tax structure, greater regulation of the financial industry and large corporations,

a reduction in military spending and foreign incursions, an overall move towards a more egalitarian society" (#122).

- "Occupy is a people's movement for Social Justice and Democracy. We are working to change the national dialogue and remove money from the Democratic Process so that all people in this country have a voice" (#268).
- "[We are] struggling to achieve greater fairness and equity between the 'have' and the 'have-nots'. Strengthening the ability of the 'non-1%' to get an education that doesn't cost an arm-and-leg" (#387).

Sustainable society

Another important topic for the respondents is the need for a sustainable society.

- Occupy has the "desire to work together to find ways of organising the world that is sustainable, fair and enriching for human lives" (#10),
- "For a sustainable economy & ecology" (#62).
- "The present economic system pollutes land, sea and air, is causing massive loss of natural species and environments, and is accelerating humanity towards irreversible climate change. We call for a positive, sustainable economic system that benefits present and future generations" (#109).

A better world

Social movements are an indication that there are fundamental problems in society. Their opponents often argue that they do not have a clear vision of an alternative society in order to silence them and to make the (incorrect) point that there are no alternatives. It is maybe too high a demand to ask social movements to come up with a blueprint of an alternative society because alternatives emerge in the process of struggle. What most activists in the Occupy movement share is a desire for a better world. "The

Occupy Movement is about the bottom majority of the country taking action in their hands to create a better world, the one we want because we are tired of waiting for the top to do it. The Federal Government is never going to save the world. We have to do it ourselves and make it happen" (#76).

Abolishment of the influence of the economy on politics

For some of the respondent, the goal is not necessarily the abolishment of capitalism or the establishment of a new society, a participatory democracy, but rather the abolishment of the strong influence the capitalist economy has on politics today.

- "Abolish corporate Personhood, corrupt banks and politicians" (#241).
- "Occupy is a "collective of like-minded individuals protesting to regain control of their government from business interest and the financial markets" (#272).
- Occupy's "point of focus [is] to demand that corporate money get out of the political processes in the USA" (#314).
- Occupy wants a revolution against corporate control of government and everything else (#342).

Accountability

A related topic is that governments, banks and corporations should be held accountable for what they do:

- Occupy is "demanding accountability from government and financial industry" (#242).
- It is "a worldwide accountability movement that draws strength from decentralized, semi-autonomous groups that seek to define, raise awareness of, and begin to achieve solutions to locally-identified problems" (#246).
- "The basic goals were to unite as many people as possible

to get corporate money out of politics, to hold financial institutions accountable for their wrongdoing, as well as the government" (#265).

Autonomy, freedom and self-determination

Another goal is to advance self-determination and freedom:

- "For me, the occupy movement is a part of the global opportunity to perform the global leap in direction towards more self-determination that is our right de jure (and morally), but not de facto" (#19).
- Occupy is "a movement for real freedom" (#169).

Raising political awareness

Some of the respondents argue that an important Occupy goal is to raise awareness about specific political issues:

- Occupy is a "movement to create awareness of inequality, injustice, poverty and the unsustainable use of natural resources" (#31).
- The task is the "active raising of consciousness about the destructive effects of capitalism and neoliberalism in particular" (#74).
- "Putting the issue of the 1% vs the 99% into the public discussion arena" (#101).
- Occupy is a "community of social activists trying to wake up humanity" (#124).
- "It's an attempt to influence mainstream media" (#148).
- The task is "reviving class consciousness in America" (#234)

The abolition of war and establishment of a peaceful society

For some respondents the establishment of a peaceful society without war is a primary goal:

- "Financial fairness, abolishment of war and world hunger" (#53).
- "The goal of promoting a sustainable, peaceful society through innovation not regression" (#198).
- Occupy wants "to achieve peace and happiness for everyone around the world" (#248).

Many respondents do not identify a single goal of the Occupy movement, but rather focus on a number of the discussed goals. For example, one respondent says that the goals are "Many respondents do not identify a single goal of the Occupy movement, but rather focus the environment from the industrial complex, and ending capitalism in its present form, by redistributing wealth" (#330)

5.2.3. Methods of Protest

In struggling against identified problems and towards defined goals, protest movements make use of certain methods. The OccupyMedia! Survey identified several protest methods of the Occupy movement:

Occupations for reclaiming public space and the public sphere (=a goal and a method)

- Occupy is protesting "mainly by reclaiming public space" (#8).
- Occupy is "a movement built solely around a tactic – to go forth and occupy shit to raise awareness of what the 99% faces" (#170).

- Occupy is "about resisting capitalism through grassroots direct action" (#12).
- Occupy engages in the "public reclamation of public space as a new praxis of politics" (#23).
- Occupy is "using public space in creative ways to make a political statement" (#51),
- Occupying is "a means to reclaim public space, public discourse and the public sphere" (#184),
- The protest method is "occupying places so that we can camp together and sing around fires" (#298).

Non-violence

- "the non-violence of the people is not a matter of cowardice or 'hippie crap' but the actual only way that can be used in order to reach the end goal as aggression discourages participants while clarifying repression builds activity" (#19).
- "A nonviolent revolution for fairness, participatory democracy, and clean, renewable energy" (#160).
- "I think our only true strategy is non violence" (#163).
- "Occupy is our only true strategy is nr. Martin Luther King, Jr. had ... He called for people-based, militant, and democratic organizations to be formed in the Western nations which would work against corporate control – and wage non-violent war TO WIN" (#312).

Humor and glamor

Performance artist Marni Halasa, who shows up in spectacular costumes at Occupy protests, says: "What I am trying to do is become a new kind of protester, changing the public view that not all protesters are unemployed, angry and hostile. I have also found that bringing a sense of humor and glamour to the movement diffuses often tense situations, which I think helps control things in the long run" (#112).

5.2.4. Forms of Organization

The most frequent statement about Occupy's form of organization is that it is a grassroots movement. There are however also critical remarks on the limits of grassroots organizations.

Occupy as a grassroots movement

- "It's a movement that tries to show the importance and the possibility of grassroots movements and grassroots democracy" (#20).
- Occupy is "creative self-organization, now on display with Occupy Sandy and the debt relief project" (#101).
- "A grassroots effort to organize against corruption inherent in both the public and private sector that negatively impacts the people" (#147).
- "It is a direct decentralized attack on a system of capitalism that makes life miserable for millions and the governance that makes it possible" (#251).
- "The grassroots character of Occupy was partly also described as an anarchist form of organization: "We come together identify common grievances, discuss possible solutions, & plan and execute tactics toward the better world our discussions have convinced us is possible. For me, that's anarchism" (#125). Occupy is "anarchist, horizontal, mutualistic" (#316).
- Occupy is "a new way of participating" (#202).
- It is "very inclusive and democratic, a place to express opinion and take decisive action" (#279).
- It is "an arena for discussion of, and action upon humanity's most serious and immediate issues. It is an experiment, not only of democracy but of direct and non-violent communication" (#398).
- Grassroots organization is also seen as the anticipation of participatory democracy as organizational form of society: Occupy is a "way to develop a participatory, grass roots

movement to organize society from the ground up" (#87), "an experiment in radical democracy" (#95).

Problems of grassroots organization

Some respondents argue that from the leaderless grassroots model a new form of leadership emerged: "It became more of a cult of personality with many large personalities involved. As media attention became more of the norm, it seemed that a core group of people were more focused on the attention than the cause. There is a deeply ingrained problem of celebrity worship in American society, and I felt that its affects manifested in the way some of the activists handled media attention" (#265).

Others say that consensus culture resulted in wasted time: "Way too much time is wasted on consensus and visioning. In my area there was way too much time wasted on every one speaking endlessly" (#119). "The Occupy movement was an experiment in mass democracy and an exploration of democratic rights. It never developed the maturity needed to have a strong 'vision' as there were competing trends within Occupy, competing 'visions'. I've heard many complaints and comments from people about being bogged down in process, with major debates of consensus vs. majority rule" (#291)

That activists, on the one hand stress the value of grassroots organization, but on the other hand mention the difficulty of practicing this form of organization reflects the scarcity of time and resources that social movements within capitalist society are facing.

A networked movement

Occupy means "networking with everyone from local interest campaigns to international groups, in an attempt to build solidarity and a movement with a realistic chance of bringing about radical change" (#13). Occupy is "a mobilizing and networking opportunity for the people to start taking responsibility for their future" (#492).

Different ways of life

Occupy means "experimenting with different ways of living and organising right now" (#13), "the camps were a way that people could imagine new ways of being together" (#28).

Occupy "is the opportunity of showing another way of life, respectful with the other as well as the environment. We are more effective than a government in many cases, we've the technology and knowledge to build an utopia, to create our own world" (#103). For some everyday life in the camp was more important for decision-making than the general assemblies: "I'd also say that the most significant organizational form of Occupy is/was the camp, not the general assembly. General Assemblies were often dysfunctional and were not the spaces where decisions were made, except in the very beginning, when people didn't know each other" (#28).

A diverse movement

- Occupy is "trying to accept and respect diversity of opinion and tactics, enabling everyone's voice to be heard and common ground to be found" (#13).
- Occupy is "a polymorphous, polysemic transnational movement" (#8).
- "For me, the Occupy movement is a horizontal revolution movement that has very diverse political points of view from its participants" (#22).
- "For me, the Occupy movement is a horizontal revolution movement that has very diverse political points of view from its participants" (#22).
- "People with diverse interests who want to make a better world" (201).

The movement's diversity would also result in the problem of fragmentation: "the movement is just too heterogeneous to describe in few words. This is, to me, its main problem" (#193).

A global movement

"It is a global movement that wants to make a better world" (#25), "a place to join forces to make change in the world. A movement with such global expanse to make the elite afraid and the ignorant/indifferent more awake!" (#59).

Mutual aid

"The tactic used, the protest camp, led to the creation of numerous proactive initiatives to provide alternatives to our current practices in the financial system and elsewhere. These were built on horizontal and open-source networks of mutual aid, at the local and international levels" (#63).

Occupy gives hope that change is possible

"Hope" (#80, #190). "For me, the Occupy movement is hopeful" (#195).

A community that gives people a voice in political engagement

- "Talking with strangers in public about politics. Waking up from consumer passive apathy and as engaged citizens. Finding and developing each person's voice. Developing community. Gathering with a diverse range of lifestyles and perspectives" (#231).
- Occupy "(was) about the right to be heard. It was about finding community" (#238).
- "Occupy is a way to free that voice and the Internet is our way to amplify it" (#251).
- Occupy is "a network of solidarity, a community of mutual

respect where anyone can have a voice" (#261).

The survey asked the respondents: "Which of the following sentences describe in your opinion the Occupy movement best?" and received 373 answers. Multiple answers were possible. Figure 2 summarizes the results.

The Occupy movement is a class struggle movement.		47.7%	178
The Occupy movement is an anti-capitalist movement.		46.9%	175
The Occupy movement is predominantly a socialist movement.		14.7%	55
The Occupy movement is predominantly a liberal movement.		13.4%	50
The Occupy movement is predominantly a movement that struggles for the common control of wealth and society.		53.1%	198
The Occupy movement is predominantly a right-wing movement.		1.9%	7
The Occupy movement is a form of social movement that is different from the working class movement, comparable to movements such as the ecological movement, the feminist movement or anti-racist movements.		40.5%	151
The Occupy movement is a networked social movement.		68.4%	255
	answered question		373

Figure 2: Activists' perception of the Occupy movement, N=373

The majority of the respondents see Occupy as a networked movement that struggles for the common control of society and wealth. There is only little agreement to the statement that Occupy is a socialist movement, whereas more than half of the respondents agree that it is a movement that struggles for a society and economy that are commonly controlled. This result shows that political terms that have historically had negative connotations – such as socialism and communism – tend not to be associated with the movement. This does however not mean that the content of these concepts is outdated, but rather that the terms themselves are unpopular. Socialism and communism are terms that for Marx and Engels indicated movements for the common control of the economy and society. Today one can say that socialism and communism mean participatory democracy, a society in which all realms of life, such as the economy and politics, are governed and controlled by those who are affected by them. It is a society that is controlled by the people in common. 54% of the respondents agreed that Occupy is predominantly a movement that struggles for the common control of society and the economy. In contrast to a commons-based society, capitalism is a society that is governed by the drive for accumulation and that is therefore controlled by the few. The process of transition from capitalism to a commons-based society is one of class struggle. The notions of class struggle, anti-capitalism, socialism and the commons are inherently connected. I therefore combined these four variables into one that shows if a respondent considers the Occupy movement as either focused on class struggle, anti-capitalism, socialism or the struggle for the commons. The variable indicates if a respondent sees Occupy as a new kind of left-wing working class movement that struggles for a classless society. The four notions of class struggle, anti-capitalism, socialism and the commons share the focus on the questioning of class. 303 out of 373 respondents (81.2%) saw Occupy as a movement that is critical of class society (see figure 3).

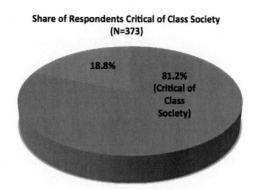

Figure 3: Respondents critical of class society, N=373

In contrast only 1.9% assessed it as being a right-wing movement and 13.4% as being a liberal movement.

5.3. Occupy and Social Media

One question in the OccupyMedia! Survey focused on the role of social media in the movement. We asked the respondents: "Which of the following statements describes best your opinion on the role of social media (such as Facebook, YouTube, Twitter, N-1, Diaspora*, Occupii) in the Occupy movement?" There were four possible answer options, a techno-deterministic one, a social constructivist one, a dialectical one and a dualistic one. The results are shown in Table 12.

	Frequency	Percent
Social media created the Occupy movement.	24	6.6
Protests and revolutions are made by humans who struggle in society, not by media or technologies. Media do not play a major role in the movement.	26	7.1
The Occupy movement is a social protest movement. Social media are tools of struggle, but also tools of domination. What the effects of social media are for Occupy and society depends on the outcome of power struggles.	166	45.5
The Occupy movement is both a social media rebellion and a rebellion in society.	149	40.8
Total	365	100.0

Table 12: The respondents' assessment of the role of social media in the Occupy movement, N=365

The data show that the respondents' most frequent assessment (45.5%) is a dialectical one, namely that social media have a contradictory character, as both tools of domination and tools of struggle and that social media use is connected to power struggles. The techno-deterministic answer option achieved the smallest agreement (6.6%), the social constructivist explanation that denies a role of social media in rebellions was almost equally dismissed with an agreement of only 7.1%.

Respondents were invited to provide additional comments about the role of social media in the Occupy movement in a text box. Some of the comments are documented below.

- "The corporate media are not our allies, we must create our own media systems" (#1).
- "Social media can be useful but technologies merely alter social-political possibilities, they do not guarantee outcomes- and the same social media that can ferment rebellion might also be used to suppress it (e.g. surveillance)" (#11).
- "I'd say that there were a number of people who felt that their best way to contribute to the movement was to spend a lot of time on Facebook and Twitter. These people were largely separate from what was actually being discussed on the ground" (#51).
- "As a member of Occupy Los Angeles social media team I see the effectiveness of media peak and fall. The classic platforms such as Facebook is certainly a tool of domination, but can be leveraged against dominance on a limited scale. I look forward to Occupy having its own platform that reaches not just the converted, but the curious" (#55).
- "Social media has been the strength and also the bane of Occupy movements everywhere" (#69).
- "Social media can mobilize, but is not the place where the real work gets done" (#87).
- "Those are tools, and must use them with responsibility as any other tool. We depend on some of them which are owned by corporations, so it's logical to create our own, we only lack some resources" (#103).
- "Social media is both a tool for social movements AND ALSO virtual spaces ARE REAL SPACES, so social media is also a space in which the movement takes places, organizes etc. It is not the only space and it is not the only tool; it is one tool and one space of the social movement" (#113).

- "The Occupy movement has made use of social media as a tool. It is not a substitute for community organizing and actions that live out the principles of the movement" (#129).
- "Social media has been used against Occupy as much as it has gained from it. Many platforms have blocked Occupy and controversial related posts. People in general are scared to leave the herd and explore new platforms and new ideas" (#157).
- "Social media are an essential tool in Occupy movements because they enable protesters to generate news instead of having to rely on mainstream media" (#184).
- "Social media had rewards but also risks. We had mentally ill and potential intelligence agents attempt to gain access to the media team, demanding rights to be allowed to use the main social media accounts on Twitter and Facebook. Live-stream users also created conflict. They didn't seem to understand the risks they were creating with their constant online sousveillance of activities around the camp" (#238).
- "Social Media played a role as tools used for networking, but in themselves did not create the conditions necessary for any uprising etc" (#291).
- "Social media (technology) has made it easier for people to get involved. Its downside is that the networks are not secure and can be used against us" (#347).
- "I feel that the risk of censorship and the presence of unlawful surveillance are both very high in current social media. Search engines are able to select which results to place higher, major media outlets don't cover what I've seen and read through social media and eyewitness videos/accounts ... Social media is a lifeline to truth and should be guarded by the people to make sure it stays free and open!" (#364).

The comments show that respondents tend to neither overestimate nor underestimate the power of social media. They are aware of both these media's potentials and limits. They point out opportunities for networking, mobilization and bypassing the mainstream media. Simultaneously they stress that there are dangers such as surveillance, censorship, separation from street protests, infiltration by the police and secret services, corporate control and a stratified visibility and attention economy. Some activists therefore point out the need for Occupy to create and control its own social media, which would face resource limits and the fact that many people are scared to leave corporate social media because they have many contacts there.

5.4. Communicating Activism

5.4.1. Protest Information

The OccupyMedia! Survey asked the respondents: "If you think back to a month, in which you were involved in Occupy protests, then how often did you use any of the following media for informing yourself about the protests and the occupation?" The question aimed at analyzing Occupy activists' cognitive use of media for informing themselves about the protests. The results are shown in Table 13. In order to improve the understandability of the results, I summarized them in the following way: infrequent usage was considered as 0-3 times per month, medium usage as 4-9 times/month and frequent usage as >9 times/month. The recoded results are shown in Table 14.

Medium	Never	1-3	4-6	7-9	>9	N
Personal conversation	5.4%	17.0%	10.8%	8.2%	58.6%	353
Television	59.9%	22.4%	5.8%	2.6%	9.3%	344
Radio	54.8%	23.8%	7.6%	2.3%	11.4%	341
Mainstream newspapers	44.2%	28.6%	7.7%	4.7%	14.7%	339
Leaflets	20.6%	32.5%	17.4%	10.4%	19.1%	345
Occupy newspapers	29.3%	34.6%	15.8%	6.2%	14.1%	341
Posters	29.0%	33.1%	16.0%	7.1%	14.8%	338
SMS	43.6%	16.4%	9.4%	7.0%	23.6%	330
Phone calls	37.8%	26.8%	10.6%	5.3%	19.5%	339
Personal emails	18.7%	18.1%	10.9%	12.9%	39.4%	348
email mailing lists	20.8%	20.2%	10.7%	8.9%	39.3%	336
Occupy live video stream	16.5%	28.1%	15.3%	10.5%	29.6%	334
Occupy websites	7.2%	17.9%	19.1%	12.8%	43.0%	335
Tumblr blog "We are the 99%"	65.2%	19.1%	6.2%	3.1%	6.5%	325
Occupy Wall Street on reddit	67.6%	15.9%	5.8%	0.9%	9.8%	327
Twitter	38.8%	9.2%	7.0%	6.4%	38.5%	327
Facebook	15.2%	9.7%	11.7%	7.9%	55.4%	341
YouTube	18.1%	21.8%	15.7%	11.2%	33.2%	331
Occupy Wiki	64.8%	18.7%	3.7%	4.7%	8.1%	321

Table 13: Frequency of usage per month of specific media for protest information in the OccupyMedia! Survey

	Infrequently (0-3 times per month)	Medium (4-9 times per month)	Frequently (>9 times per month)
Personal conversation	22.40%	19.00%	58.60%
Television	82.30%	8.40%	9.30%
Radio	78.60%	9.90%	11.40%
Mainstream newspapers	72.80%	12.40%	14.70%
Leaflets	53.10%	27.80%	19.10%
Occupy newspapers	63.90%	22.00%	14.10%
Posters	62.10%	23.10%	14.80%
SMS	60.00%	16.40%	23.60%
Phone calls	64.60%	15.90%	19.50%
Personal emails	36.80%	23.80%	39.40%
Email mailing lists	41.00%	19.60%	39.30%
Occupy live video stream	44.60%	25.80%	29.60%
Occupy websites	25.10%	31.90%	43.00%
Tumblr blog "We are the 99%"	84.30%	9.30%	6.50%
Occupy Wall Street on reddit	83.50%	6.70%	9.80%
Twitter	48.00%	13.40%	38.50%
Facebook	24.90%	19.60%	55.40%
YouTube	39.90%	26.90%	33.20%
Occupy Wiki	83.50%	8.40%	8.10%

Table 14: Frequency of usage per month of specific media for protest information in the OccupyMedia! Survey

The data shows that the personal face-to-face conversation is the form of communication most frequently used by Occupy for obtaining information about the protests. Facebook is also very important as a source of information, but a little less important than the personal conversation. Other important sources of information are Occupy websites, personal emails, email mailing lists,

Twitter and YouTube. The data indicates that digital media are much more important information sources than traditional media (phone, newspapers, TV, radio). Essential digital media information sources include both newer media (Twitter, Facebook, YouTube) as well as well-established ones (email, mailing lists, web sites). The social media use for information purposes is concentrated on the three most popular sites (Facebook, Twitter, YouTube), whereas lesser-known media (such as the Occupy Wiki, reddit, Tumblr) are rather used infrequently.

I used Spearman's rho for calculating basic correlations between the intensity of activism and political positioning on the one hand and the intensity of media use for information purposes on the other hand. The results are shown in Table 15. There is a highly significant positive correlation between the intensity of activism and the frequency of the usage of personal conversations, radio, newspapers, leaflets, posters, SMS, phones, emails, video live streams, Twitter, Facebook and YouTube for information purposes. There are no significant correlations between political attitude and information frequency. This can be explained by the circumstance that our respondents are politically relatively homogenous: the very large majority was politically very left-leaning, there was only a small share of right-wing respondents.

	Intensity of activism, significance	Political positioning, significance
Occupy Wiki	0.091, 0.105	0.062, 0.267
YouTube	0.290**, 0.000	0.103, 0.060
Facebook	0.317**, 0.000	0.014, 0.796
Twitter	0.253**, 0.000	-0.015, 0.785
reddit	0.056, 0.309	0.089, 0.106
Tumblr 99%	-0.025, 0.657	0.042, 0.456
Occupy websites	0.372**, 0.000	-0.015, 0.787
Video live streams	0.271**, 0.000	0.012, 0.822
Mailing lists	0.463**, 0.000	0.019, 0.730
Emails	0.546**, 0.000	0.002, 0.974
Phone calls	0.508**, 0.000	-0.011, 0.845
SMS	0.432**, 0.000	0.049, 0.374
Posters	0.484**, 0.000	-0.012, 0.828
Occupy newspapers	0.417**, 0.000	-0.018, 0.744
Leaflets	0.534**, 0.000	-0.073, 0.178
Mainstream newspapers	0.216**, 0.000	0.047, 0.386
Radio	0.159**, 0.003	0.042, 0.441
TV	0.028, 0.602	0.053, 0.329
Personal conversation	0.528**, 0.000	0.045, 0.400

Table 15: Correlations between information frequency and activism intensity, political positioning, personal conversation frequency, Facebook usage frequency (Spearman's rho)

	Personal conversations, significance	Facebook usage frequency, significance
Occupy Wiki	0.135*, 0.015	0.196**, 0.000
YouTube	0.376**, 0.000	0.510**, 0.000
Facebook	0.325**, 0.000	-
Twitter	0.215**, 0.000	0.333*, 0.000
reddit	0.074, 0.183	0.045, 0.416
Tumblr 99%	0.104, 0.061	0.087, 0.120
Occupy websites	0.458**,	0.339*, 0.000
Video live streams	0.382**,	0.276**, 0.000
Mailing lists	0.445**,	0.297**, 0.000
Emails	0.529**,	0.273**, 0.000
Phone calls	0.448**,	0.239**, 0.000
SMS	0.350**,	0.327**, 0.000
Posters	0.456**, 0.000	0.265**, 0.000
Occupy newspapers	0.392**, 0.000	0.212**, 0.000
Leaflets	0.457**, 0.000	0.253**, 0.000
Mainstream newspapers	0.282**, 0.000	0.129*, 0.019
Radio	0.234**, 0.000	0.032, 0.564
TV	0.095, 0.078	0.014, 0.805
Personal conversation	-	0.325**, 0.000

Table 15: continued.

A higher number of personal conversations about protests tends to result in a more frequent use of radio, newspapers, leaflets, posters, phones, emails, video streams, Occupy websites, Twitter, Facebook and YouTube. More frequent Facebook usage correlates with more frequent personal conversations and more frequent usage of newspapers, posters, SMS, phones, emails, live streams, Occupy websites, YouTube and the Occupy Wiki for information purposes. This shows that the two most frequent information sources, personal conversations and Facebook, mutually amplify each other and also amplify the usage of other media. There is no substitution of one form of information by another, but rather a mutual reinforcement of diverse political information sources in the Occupy movement.

5.4.2. User-Generated Protest Content

The Internet not only allows users to access information others have published online, but also to create content themselves. The question that arises is to what extent Occupy activists engage in the creation of user-generated content about the movement. To find out, we asked the respondents in the OccupyMedia! Survey: "If you think back to a month, in which you were involved in Occupy protests, then how often did you yourself or together with others create content about the Occupy movement that you shared online?". The results are shown in detail in Table 16 and in simplified form in Table 17.

	Never	1-3	4-6	7-9	>9	N
I took pictures and shared them on Flickr	82.8%	8.9%	2.8%	1.2%	4.3%	326
I took pictures and shared them in a Facebook Occupy group	51.1%	17.1%	11.7%	1.8%	18.3%	333
I shared pictures on an alternative social networking site (Diaspora*, N-1, Occupii, etc)	76.8%	10.5%	3.4%	2.5%	6.8%	323
I created a YouTube video	71.5%	21.8%	2.4%	0.3%	3.9%	330
I took videos and shared them on Facebook	66.5%	13.8%	7.7%	1.2%	10.8%	325
I took videos and shared them on an alternative social networking site	84.6%	7.7%	1.8%	0.6%	5.2%	325
I wrote a blog post about the Occupy movement on my own blog	61.3%	20.4%	7.0%	4.0%	7.3%	328
I wrote a blog post or news entry for an Occupy website	62.6%	17.3%	6.7%	3.0%	10.3%	329
I posted an image story on the Tumblr blog "We are the 99 percent"	93.1%	5.0%	0.3%	0.6%	0.9%	319
I contributed to the Occupy Wiki	89.1%	6.2%	1.6%	1.2%	1.9%	322
I helped setting up or maintaining an Occupy live video stream	75.6%	12.7%	3.1%	0.9%	7.7%	324

Table 16: Frequency of usage per month of specific social media for creating user-generated content about the Occupy movement

	Never	1-3	4-6	7-9	>9	N
I posted news on the occupywallstreet page of the social news service reddit	92.2%	4.7%	0.9%	0.6%	1.6%	319
I helped programming software that was used by the Occupy movement	89.3%	5.6%	0.6%	1.3%	3.1%	319
I helped designing websites of the Occupy movement	74.5%	14.0%	3.4%	0.9%	7.2%	321
I worked as administrator of an Occupy website	69.1%	8.8%	3.5%	1.6%	17.0%	317
I helped creating podcasts (e.g. for Occupy Radio)	91.1%	5.7%	0.6%	0.6%	1.9%	316
I helped creating a newspaper for the movement (e.g. Occupied Wall Street Journal, Occupied Times of London, Occupied Chicago Tribute, DC Mic Check, etc)	83.0%	10.1%	1.9%	0.9%	4.1%	317
I worked in one of the movements' news services (e.g. Occupy News Network, member of an Occupy press group)	76.6%	7.5%	4.7%	2.5%	8.8%	320
I helped creating online guidelines for protest practices (e.g. on http://howtooccupy.org)	82.4%	9.7%	2.2%	1.9%	3.8%	318

Table 16: Continued

	Infrequently (0 times per month)	Medium (1-6)	Frequently (>6)
I took pictures and shared them on Flickr	82.80%	11.70%	5.50%
I took pictures and shared them in a Facebook Occupy group	51.10%	28.80%	20.10%
I shared pictures on an alternative social networking sites (Diaspora*, N-1, Occupii, etc)	76.80%	13.90%	9.30%
I created a YouTube video	71.50%	24.20%	4.20%
I took videos and shared them on Facebook	66.50%	21.50%	12.00%
I took videos and shared them on an alternative social networking site	84.60%	9.50%	5.80%
I wrote a blog post about the Occupy movement on my own blog	61.30%	27.40%	11.30%
I wrote a blog post or news entry for an Occupy website	62.60%	24.00%	13.30%
I posted an image story on the Tumblr blog "We are the 99 percent"	93.10%	5.30%	1.50%
I contributed to the Occupy Wiki	89.10%	7.80%	3.10%

Table 17: Frequency of usage per month of specific social media for creating user-generated content about the Occupy movement

	Infrequently (0 times per month)	Medium (1-6)	Frequently (>6)
I helped setting up or maintaining an Occupy live video stream	75.60%	15.80%	8.60%
I posted news on the occupywallstreet page of the social news service reddit	92.20%	5.60%	2.20%
I helped programming software that was used by the Occupy movement	89.30%	6.20%	4.40%
I helped designing websites of the Occupy movement	74.50%	17.40%	8.10%
I worked as administrator of an Occupy website	69.10%	12.30%	18.60%
I helped creating podcasts (e.g. for Occupy Radio)	91.10%	6.30%	2.50%
I helped creating a newspaper for the movement (e.g. Occupied Wall Street Journal, Occupied Times of London, Occupied Chicago Tribune, DC Mic Check, etc)	83.00%	12.00%	5.00%
I worked in one of the movements' news services (e.g. Occupy News Network, member of an Occupy press group)	76.60%	12.20%	11.30%
I helped creating online guidelines for protest practices (e.g. on http://howtooccupy.org)	82.40%	11.90%	5.70%

Table 17: Continued.

The tables show that a large majority of the respondents in the OccupyMedia! Survey very infrequently created and shared content about Occupy online. Depending on the activity, between 51.1% and 93.1% of the respondents never created and shared content online. The rather easy task of taking pictures and uploading them on Flickr, Facebook or another social medium, was the most frequently conducted form of user-generated content creation: 17.1% conducted this task on Facebook 1-3 times per month, 11.7% 4-6 times, 20.1% more than 6 times. 51.1% never performed this task on Facebook. More complex tasks such as sharing a video on YouTube were more infrequent: 71.5% never conducted this task, 21.8% 1-3 times per month, 2.4% 4-6 times, 4.2% more than 6 times.

If we consider frequent content creation to mean at least 7 times per month, then the share of frequently active users is 20.1% for sharing pictures on Facebook, 18.6% for working as administrator for an Occupy website, 13.3% for writing blog posts on an Occupy site, 12.0% for sharing videos on Facebook, 11.3% for working for one of the movements' news services, 11.3% for writing posts on a personal blog, 9.3% for sharing pictures on an alternative social networking site and 8.6% for helping to operate a live video feed. The data show that it seems to be a smaller group of around 10-20% of the activists that specializes in social media activism and makes use of technologies such as video live feeds, social networking sites, blogs, video sharing and alternative news services.

Another result is that dominant corporate social media are used more frequently for sharing user-generated content than alternative social media: 48.9% of the respondents shared images on Facebook at least once a month, whereas only 23.2% did so on an alternative social medium (such as Diaspora*, N-1, Occupii). 33.5% shared videos about Occupy on Facebook at least once a month, but only 15.4% on an alternative platform. An interesting result is that the share of respondents who worked as group or site administrators at least once a month was 30.9%. This is an indication that it is a common practice that Occupy groups share the administration and login data of profiles and accounts on social media among a certain group of activists so that they obtain higher visibility in the public by allowing a group of people to post. 24.4% of the respondents helped operate a video live stream of the Occupy movement at least once a month. This result is interesting because it shows that a significant share of activists helped with setting up and operating live streams, which is an indication that this form of communication has been particularly important for the Occupy movement.

A result that is not shown in detail in the tables, but that correlation analysis of the dataset shows is that most user-generated content creation activities strongly correlate with each other at a significant level. So for example the frequency of creating YouTube videos correlates strongly with all other frequencies of activities that produce user-generated content. This result shows that Occupy's social media activists do not concentrate their activities on a single platform or media, but engage in posting content on a broad range of platforms such as blogs, social networking sites, video sharing sites, live video feeds, alternative news services, wikis, etc.

The results presented in Table 18 show that the intensity of activism is significantly positively correlated with the frequency of most user-generated content creation activities. This means that the more time one spends protesting, the more likely it is that one becomes an activist who engages in active and creative social media use. There is no significant correlation between political positioning on a left-right scale and the frequency of user-generated content creation. Here, once again the circumstance that the respondents were overall politically quite homogenous because the Occupy movement is a left-wing movement has to be taken into account.

	Intensity of activism, significance	Political positioning, significance
Online protest guidelines	0.287**, 0.000	0.055, 0.326
Movement news service	0.366*, 0.000	0.072, 0.202
Movement newspaper	0.360**, 0.000	0.086, 0.128
Podcasts	0.271**, 0.000	0.031, 0.588
Administrator, Occupy site	0.427**, 0.000	0.099, 0.077
Website design	0.392**, 0.000	0.056, 0.314
Software engineering	0.118, 0.035	0.063, 0.261
Occupy on reddit	0.050, 0.377	0.100, 0.075
Tumblr "We are the 99%"	0.121*, 0.031	-0.017, 0.758
Occupy live video stream	0.442**, 0.000	0.104, 0.061
Occupy wiki	0.125*, 0.025	0.064, 0.252
Blog post, Occupy website	0.399**, 0.000	0.132*, 0.016
Blog post, own blog	0.155**, 0.000	0.065, 0.241
Videos, alternative SNS	0.231**, 0.000	0.103, 0.064
Pictures, alternative SNS	0.205**, 0.000	0.036, 0.518
Video, Facebook	0.363**, 0.000	0.073, 0.190
Pictures, Facebook Occupy	0.395**, 0.000	0.047, 0.394
Pictures, Flickr	0.094, 0.090	0.097, 0.081
YouTube video	0.400**, 0.000	0.050, 0.368

Table 18: Correlations between the frequency of user-generated content creation and activism intensity as well as political positioning (Spearman's rho)

5.4.3. Activist Communication

A further important dimension of social movements' knowledge structures is how activists communicate with each other. In order to find out, the OccupyMedia! Survey contained the question: "If you think back to a month, in which you were involved in Occupy protests, then how often did you use any of the following media for communicating or discussing the protests with other activists?" The results are shown in Tables 19 and 20.

	Never	1-3	4-6	7-9	>9	N
Personal conversation	6.3%	18.6%	6.3%	8.2%	60.6%	317
SMS	42.5%	15.4%	8.4%	6.4%	27.4%	299
Phone calls	30.9%	24.0%	12.9%	8.5%	23.7%	317
Personal emails	17.8%	23.6%	11.1%	10.8%	36.6%	314
Email mailing lists	31.2%	18.5%	10.4%	7.5%	32.5%	308
Occupy movement chat	48.4%	21.6%	11.0%	3.9%	15.2%	310
Twitter	44.1%	12.2%	6.1%	5.1%	32.5%	311
Facebook group	24.9%	12.3%	8.5%	8.8%	45.4%	317
YouTube comments	61.5%	18.4%	8.9%	2.3%	8.9%	304
Riseup communication tools	74.2%	9.2%	4.6%	3.3%	8.8%	306
InterOccupy teleconferences	76.0%	14.4%	4.8%	1.0%	3.8%	312
OccupyTalk voice chat	90.6%	4.9%	1.0%	0.3%	3.3%	307

Table 19: Frequency of usage per month of specific social media for communicating or discussing the protests with other activists

	Infrequently (0-3)	Medium (4-8)	Frequently (>9)
Personal conversation	24.90%	14.50%	60.60%
SMS	57.90%	14.80%	27.40%
Phone calls	54.90%	21.40%	23.70%
Personal emails	41.40%	21.90%	36.60%
Email mailing lists	49.70%	17.90%	32.50%
Occupy movement chat	70.00%	14.90%	15.20%
Twitter	56.30%	11.20%	32.50%
Facebook group	37.20%	17.30%	45.40%
YouTube comments	79.90%	11.20%	8.90%
Riseup communi- cation tools	83.40%	7.90%	8.80%
InterOccupy teleconfe- rences	90.40%	5.80%	3.80%
OccupyTalk voice chat	95.50%	1.30%	3.30%

Table 20: Frequency of usage per month of specific social media for communicating or discussing the protests with other activists

The data provides indications that the personal conversation is the most frequent form of communication in the Occupy movement, followed by communication on Facebook, email, mailing lists and Twitter. SMS and mobile phones were less frequently used for movement communication than face-to-face communication, email and social media (Facebook, Twitter). The question on movement communication contained a field that allowed respondents to add additional communication channels that are important for them. They mentioned e.g. Mumble,

Skype, Google+, Google Hangouts, Yahoo Messenger, Revleft.com, Iopsociety.org. Using Spearman's rho, I conducted a correlation analysis of the Occupy protest communication variables. The results are presented in Table 21.

	Intensity of activism, significance	Political positioning, significance	Personal conversation, significance
OccupyTalk	0.177**, 0.002	0.102, 0.075	0.013, 0.820
InterOccupy teleconferences	0.346**, 0.000	0.019, 0.735	0.157*, 0.006
Riseup	0.314**, 0.000	-0.037, 0.522	0.149**, 0.009
YouTube	0.161**, 0.005	0.036, 0.537	0.194**, 0.001
Facebook	0.375**, 0.000	0.077, 0.169	0.243**, 0.000
Twitter	0.304**, 0.000	-0.012, 0.828	0.209**, 0.000
Occupy movement chat	0.312**, 0.000	0.061, 0.285	0.272**, 0.000
Email mailing lists	0.417**, 0.000	-0.019, 0.737	0.367**, 0.000
Personal emails	0.515**, 0.000	-0.065, 0.254	0.540**, 0.000
Phone calls	0.495**, 0.000	-0.050, 0.379	0.520**, 0.000
SMS	0.442**, 0.000	0.039, 0.503	0.392**, 0.000
Personal conversation	0.532**, 0.000	-0.013, 0.824	-

Table 21: Correlations between frequency of specific forms of protest communication for discussion, activism intensity as well as political positioning (Spearman's rho)

	Facebook, significance	Email mailing lists, significance	Twitter, significance
OccupyTalk	0.182**, 0.001	0.176**, 0.002	0.180**, 0.002
InterOccupy teleconferences	0.261**, 0.000	0.256**, 0.000	0.246**, 0.000
Riseup	0.116*, 0.043	0.301**, 0.000	0.207**, 0.000
YouTube	0.397**, 0.000	0.179**, 0.002	0.338**, 0.000
Facebook	-	0.289**, 0.000	0.313**, 0.000
Twitter	0.313**, 0.000	0.228**, 0.000	-
Occupy movement chat	0.333**, 0.000	0.211**, 0.000	0.233**, 0.000
Email mailing lists	0.289**, 0.000	-	0.228**, 0.000
Personal emails	0.338**, 0.000	0.740**, 0.000	0.203**, 0.000
Phone calls	0.251 **, 0.000	0.502**, 0.000	0.176**, 0.002
SMS	0.348**, 0.000	0.448**, 0.000	0.398**, 0.000
Personal conversation	0.243**, 0.000	0.367**, 0.000	0.209**, 0.000

Table 21: Continued

Correlation analysis shows that the intensity of activism is positively correlated with the frequency of all forms of protest communication at a significant level. The political positioning of the respondents does in contrast not correlate with their protest communication frequency. People who are more active in protests tend to engage more in communication with other activists in personal conversations, on the phone, in email mailing lists, chats, on Twitter, Facebook, YouTube and other communication media. Correlation analysis also shows that different forms of protest communication do not substitute, but complement each other: the frequency of personal communications is significantly positively correlated with the frequency of most other forms of protest communication, the frequencies of the use of Facebook, Twitter, email mailing lists and other online media for protest communication are significantly positively correlated with each other. Note that the respondents were activists, so these results say nothing about the role of social media in inhibiting or supporting the mobilization of protestors. They rather show that Occupy activists tend to make use of multiple forms of online and offline media for communicating about the protests with other activists and that these forms of protest communication tend to complement each other.

5.4.4. Mobilization Communication

Another important dimension of protest interaction is the use of media for organizing and co-ordinating protests as well as for mobilizing activists. In order to find out what role social media play in this respect in the Occupy movement, the OccupyMedia! Survey contained one question that asked the respondents: "If you think back to a month, in which you were involved in Occupy protests, then how often did you engage in certain media activities for trying to mobilise people for a protest event, discussion, demonstration or the occupation of a square, building, house or other space?" The results are shown in Tables 22 and 23.

	Never	1-3	4-6	7-9	>9	N
I had a personal face-to-face conversation in order to mobilize others	15.0%	23.5%	14.1%	8.2%	39.2%	306
I sent an email to personal contacts	29.8%	27.8%	12.6%	5.0%	24.8%	302
I phoned people	36.9%	28.2%	11.3%	3.3%	20.3%	301
I sent an SMS to my contacts	49.7%	17.9%	9.1%	5.4%	17.9%	296
I posted an announcement on an email list	46.2%	16.9%	13.0%	5.3%	18.6%	301
I posted an announcement on my Facebook profile	25.2%	20.5%	11.9%	7.6%	34.4%	302
I posted an announcement on Facebook friends' profiles	53.1%	15.3%	5.8%	3.7%	22.1%	294
I posted an announcement in an Occupy group on Facebook	44.0%	12.8%	7.7%	5.4%	30.2%	298
I posted an announcement on Twitter	52.0%	9.8%	6.1%	4.7%	27.4%	296
I created an announcement video on YouTube	85.9%	9.1%	2.0%	0.0%	3.0%	297
I posted an announcement on my own profile on the social networking site Occupii	86.1%	7.4%	2.0%	0.7%	3.7%	296
I posted an announcement on friends' profiles on the social networking site Occupii	91.3%	6.4%	1.0%	0.3%	1.0%	298
I posted an announcement in an Occupy group on the social networking site Occupii	85.3%	10.0%	1.0%	0.7%	3.0%	300
I posted an announcement on my own profile on the social networking site N-1	90.9%	4.9%	1.0%	0.7%	2.4%	143

Table 22: Frequency of usage per month of specific forms of communication in the mobilization of protest

	Never	1-3	4-6	7-9	>9	N
I posted an announcement on friends' profiles on the social networking site N-1	93.3%	3.9%	0.7%	0.4%	1.8%	282
I posted an announcement in an Occupy group on the social networking site N-1	93.9%	3.2%	0.4%	0.7%	1.8%	278
I posted an announcement on my own profile on the social networking site Diaspora*	94.3%	4.3%	0.4%	0.7%	0.4%	281
I posted an announcement on friends' profiles on the social networking site Diaspora*	95.7%	2.8%	0.7%	0.4%	0.4%	281
I posted an announcement in an Occupy group on the social networking site Diaspora*	95.7%	2.5%	0.7%	0.4%	0.7%	278
I wrote an announcement on a blog	69.0%	17.6%	4.6%	3.9%	4.9%	284
I informed people on meetup.com	87.5%	8.2%	2.5%	0.7%	1.1%	279
I informed others by using one of the movement's chats	73.8%	12.4%	5.0%	2.5%	6.4%	282
I posted an announcement on one of the movement's discussion forums	67.6%	14.2%	7.8%	2.5%	7.8%	281
I made an announcement with the help of a Riseup tool (chat, email lists)	84.7%	8.2%	2.8%	1.1%	3.2%	281
I made an announcement on an InterOccupy teleconference	86.1%	7.1%	3.9%	0.7%	2.1%	281
I announced something on OccupyTalk voice chat	95.3%	1.8%	1.1%	0.0%	1.8%	279

Table 22: Continued.

	Infrequently (0)	Medium (1-6)	Frequently (>6)
I had a personal face-to-face conversation in order to mobilize others	15.0%	37.60%	47.40%
I sent an email to personal contacts	29.8%	40.40%	29.80%
I phoned people	36.9%	39.50%	23.60%
I sent an SMS to my contacts	49.7%	27.00%	23.30%
I posted an announcement on an email list	46.2%	29.90%	23.90%
I posted an announcement on my Facebook profile	25.2%	32.40%	42.00%
I posted an announcement on Facebook friends' profiles	53.1%	21.10%	25.80%
I posted an announcement in an Occupy group on Facebook	44.0%	20.50%	35.60%
I posted an announcement on Twitter	52.0%	15.90%	32.10%
I created an announcement video on YouTube	85.9%	11.10%	3.00%
I posted an announcement on my own profile on the social networking site Occupii	86.1%	9.40%	4.40%
I posted an announcement on friends' profiles on the social networking site Occupii	91.3%	7.40%	1.30%
I posted an announcement in an Occupy group on the social networking site Occupii	85.3%	11.00%	3.70%
I posted an announcement on my own profile on the social networking site N-1	90.9%	5.90%	3.10%
I posted an announcement on friends' profiles on the SNS N-1	93.3%	4.60%	2.20%

Table 23: Frequency of usage per month of specific forms of communication in the mobilization of protest

The data indicates that face-to-face communication, Facebook, email, phone, SMS and Twitter are the most important media that

	Infrequently (0)	Medium (1-6)	Frequently (>6)
I posted an announcement in an Occupy group on the social networking site N-1	93.9%	3.60%	2.50%
I posted an announcement on my own profile on the social networking site Diaspora*	94.3%	4.70%	1.10%
I posted an announcement on friends' profiles on the social networking site Diaspora*	95.7%	3.50%	0.80%
I posted an announcement in an Occupy group on the social networking site Diaspora*	95.7%	3.20%	1.10%
I wrote an announcement on a blog	69.0%	22.20%	8.80%
I informed people on meetup.com	87.5%	10.70%	1.80%
I informed others by using one of the movement's chats	73.8%	17.40%	8.90%
I posted an announcement on one of the movement's discussion forums	67.6%	22.00%	10.30%
I made an announcement with the help of a Riseup tool (chat, email lists)	84.7%	11.00%	4.30%
I made an announcement on an InterOccupy teleconference	86.1%	11.00%	2.80%
I made an announcement with the help of the OccupyTalk voice chat	95.3%	2.90%	1.80%

Table 23: Continued.

Occupy activists employ for trying to mobilize others for protests. Activists use multiple media for mobilization-oriented communication. These include classical interpersonal communication via phones, email, face-to-face and private social media profiles as well as more public forms of communication such as Facebook groups, Twitter and email lists. Posting announcements on alternative social media is much more uncommon than doing the same on Twitter and Facebook: Whereas 42% of the respondents posted protest announcements frequently on their Facebook profiles, only 4.4% did so on Occupii, 3.1% on N-1 and 1.1% on Diaspora*. 25.8% frequently posted protest announcements on their friends' Facebook profiles, whereas only 1.3% did so on Occupii, 2.2% on N-1 and 0.8% on Diaspora*. 35.6% frequently posted protest announcements on Occupy pages/groups on Facebook, 3.7% on Occupii, 2.5% on N-1, 1.1% on Diaspora*. The data indicates that the big corporate social media are more attractive for activists in mobilization communication. The reason could be that these platforms have a large number of users and that the activists have a relatively large contact network there, whereas alternative social media are not used that much and as a consequence tend to feature smaller contact networks. Although there are various forms of protest mobilization communication, one should not overestimate this form of communication. There is a significant share of respondents who did not engage in mobilization communication: 29.8% of the respondents never sent mobilization messages via email, 36.9% never did the same via the phone, 49.7% never via SMS, 46.2% never via email lists, 44.0% never posted announcement on Facebook groups, 53.1% never wrote such messages on Facebook profiles of their friends, 52.0% never used Twitter for this purpose. There is a significantly large share of activists who engage in protest mobilization communication, but this type of communication is, although fairly common, not common to all activists.

I also conducted a correlation analysis of the variables that cover protest mobilization communication. Some of the correlation results are presented in Table 24.

	Intensity of activism, significance	Political positioning
OccupyTalk	0.072, 0.232	0.72, 0.233
InterOccupy teleconference	0.283**, 0.000	0.100, 0.093
Riseup tool	0.290**, 0.000	0.013, 0.832
Movement discussion forum	0.335**, 0.000	0.096, 0.108
Movement online chat	0.313**, 0.000	0.029, 0.632
Meetup.com	0.066, 0.274	0.151*, 0.01
Blog post	0.225**, 0.000	-0.078, 0.190
Occupy group on Diaspora*	0.059, 0.329	0.035, 0.561
Friends' profiles on Diaspora*	-0.004, 0.941	0.054, 0.369
Own profile on Diaspora*	0.020, 0.734	0.086, 0.153
Occupy group on N-1	0.101, 0.092	0.184**, 0.002
Friends' profiles on N-1	0.019, 0.748	0.160**, 0.007
Own profile on N-1	0.006, 0.926	0.123*, 0.038
Occupy group on Occupii	0.159**, 0.006	0.106, 0.067
Friends' profiles on Occupii	0.085, 0.143	0.115*, 0.047
Own profile on Occupii	0.128*, 0.028	0.027, 0.644
Video on YouTube	0.294**, 0.000	0.026, 0.660
Twitter	0.340**, 0.000	0.030, 0.605
Occupy group on FB	0.481**, 0.000	0.125*, 0.031
Friends' FB profiles	0.307**, 0.000	0.080, 0.171
My Facebook profile	0.337**, 0.000	0.061, 0.288
Email mailing lists	0.431**, 0.000	0.043, 0.460
SMS	0.389**, 0.000	0.074, 0.206
Phone calls	0.428**, 0.000	-0.011, 0.856
Personal email	0.443**, 0.000	-0.103, 0.075
Personal conversation	0.497**, 0.000	-0.092, 0.109

Table 24: Correlations between the frequency of specific forms of protest mobilization communication, activism intensity as well as political positioning (Spearman's rho)

Correlation analysis shows that a higher level of protest activity tends to result in a higher level of media use for protest mobilization. Political positioning does not have a lot of influence on the media use in protest mobilization, with the exception of announcements on N-1. Mobilization in face-to-face communication tends to positively influence other forms of mobilization communication, with the exception of non-commercial social media platforms such as Occupii, N-1 and Diaspora*. Posting announcements on Facebook in order to mobilize others tends to positively impact other forms of mobilization communication, with the exception of some of the non-commercial platforms. Posting videos on YouTube for mobilization tends to have positive effects on the frequency of all other analyzed forms of mobilization communication. Usage of the non-commercial platform Occupii for mobilization communication tends to positively influence usage of most other forms of online communication on commercial and non-commercial platforms. It does not have positive impact on the usage of face-to-face and phone communication for mobilization.

5.5. Corporate and Alternative Social Media

Research Question 4 (Which advantages and disadvantages do Occupy activists see in relation to the movement's use of commercial digital media and alternative, non-commercial, non-profit digital media?) was operationalized by nine survey questions focusing on perceived advantages and disadvantages of commercial and non-commercial social media, what the best organization model is for alternative social media, how much activists are willing to donate per month for non-commercial social media and work for alternative social media.

The questions focusing on advantages and disadvantages of commercial and non-commercial social media were open-response questions. The qualitative results were coded with a coding scheme that was applied in such a way that not just one, but multiple codes could be applied to one answer. The result tables presented below are based on the share of answers that represent specific codes.

5.5.1. Risks of Corporate Social Media

One open survey question asked if the respondents see risks of commercial social media. Table 25 shows that 55.9% (157) argue that the main problem activists face when using commercial social media is surveillance. 22.8% (64) respondents formulate this in more general terms, encompassing both corporate and police surveillance and to a certain degree also surveillance of users by other users. 33.1% (93) say that they have major concerns about police surveillance of activists on social media. Further important concerns are that commercial platforms censor activists' content and communications, that corporations dominate social media and often hold monopoly status. 22.8% of the respondents indicate that there are only advantages.

Risk	Frequency	Share (%)
Surveillance (can be corporate and/or police surveillance and/or by other individuals/groups)	157	55.9%
Police surveillance	93	33.1%
None	64	22.8%
Censorship	32	11.4%
Corporate control/monopoly	22	7.8%
Slacktivism	6	2.1%
Trolling	6	2.1%
Communication problems	4	1.4%
Right-wing users and attackers	3	1.1%
Digital divide	3	1.1%
Hacking	2	0.7%
Trivialization of information	1	0.4%
Fragmentation of communication	1	0.4%

Table 25: Identified risks of Occupy's use of commercial social media, N=281

Here are examples for the concerns expressed about police surveillance of social media:

- "Yes – I know that police monitor these sites, especially Facebook and Twitter and they have successfully subpoenaed data from users" (#28).
- "Yes, the messages can be manipulated by others, filtered .... But the commercial platforms are necessary ... [in order to] to reach the maximum of society" (#127).
- "Yes. It risks our data being given/sold to government agencies and used against a peaceful movement. If I had my way, all forms of protest communications would be on non-commercial platforms!" (#196).
- "Privacy [violations] and governmental intervention are the main risks. If only it weren't so damned convenient to use them" (#201).
- "Yes, my Twitter account was subpoena'd, for tweeting a hashtag. The subpoena was dropped in court" (#238).
- "Being followed around town by the police and having agents show up at my work and my house are all problematic. Seeing people I care about facing years in prison over FBI entrapment cases and hearing stories of abuse is difficult" (#265).
- "Individuals I have supported have had Facebook accounts suspended, tweets catalogued as evidence against them, and this available information used for police to pre-emptively arrest them" (#270).
- "We take it for granted that we are being watched. ... Some of us that have been activists for many years, such as in the U.S. anti war movement, have been constantly infiltrated by police and take it for granted that EVERY form of communication [...] is harvested and monitored" (#330).
- I had "'friendship' requests from police forces representatives" (#417).

Some respondents mention they are aware that it is likely that the police monitor the movement:

- "The cops know everything we email everywhere. Or at least I always assume they do. I assume they're reading this. (Hey, Mr./Ms. Spy! All you ever hear us talking about is building a more democratic, more just society. You have kids. You have friends who've been cheated by the system. Don't YOU want a better world for them?)" (#163).
- "In Greece we all know that we're being monitored by the authorities even if we have nothing to hide. My (home, landline) phone is tapped, so I don't really care if Twitter may give my personal details to the police, since I know the police already have them" (#184).
- "We are completely aware that NSA, CIA, FBI and the local police monitor the movement. This way there is nothing they can tell a judge, politician, or any official that anything we do is a surprise. They know it all ahead of time" (#260).

The Center for Media and Democracy's report *Dissent or Terror* (Hodai 2013) has published indications that US counter-terrorist agencies have monitored and infiltrated the Occupy movement. This included the surveillance of activists' social media profiles, the purchase and use of special online surveillance and analysis software, the use of facial recognition software in combination with police databases for trying to identify Occupy activists who were not suspected of having committed crimes on photos obtained from Facebook. The report shows that the concerns voiced by activists in the OccupyMedia! Survey seems to be grounded in actual state practices. The report shows evidence that US state institutions perceived Occupy activists as potential terrorists, which brings up the question if the preventive monitoring of social media violates the constitutional freedoms of assembly and speech.

In an interview on *Democracy Now!* Matthew Rothschild, editor and publisher of 'The Progressive', concluded, after having read the documents that the report is based on, that there has been a "coordination going on between the police departments to crush the Occupy movement".[3] He also concluded "that law enforcement and Homeland Security have equated protesters, left-wing protesters, as terrorists. They have diverted enormous amounts of resources from counterterrorism efforts to spy on these local protesters, and then they've collaborated with the private sector, some of the very institutions – banks – that these protesters were aiming at. And as you read in that statement from the Phoenix Police Department, the effort was to mitigate these protests. I mean, why is law enforcement, why is Homeland Security, in the business of mitigating protests?"[4]

The Documents leaked by Edward Snowden revealed the existence of a large-scale surveillance programme named PRISM that is operated by the US government. Some basic facts about this programme are:

- According to the leaked documents, the NSA in the PRISM programme obtained direct access to user data from eight online/ICT companies: Aol, Apple, Facebook, Google, Microsoft, Paltalk, Skype and Yahoo. The XKeyscore program allows the NSA to monitor users' emails, visited websites, searches, metadata and social media use by specifying in an online form a user's e-mail or other online ID (name, IP address, telephone number etc).[5] The Powerpoint slides that Edward Snowden leaked talk about collection "directly from the servers of these U.S. Service Providers".
- The NSA's Director James Clapper confirmed the existence of PRISM and defended its existence.[6]

- Edward Snowden says that at the NSA "communications are collected and viewed on a daily basis", including "the content of your communications".[7]
- In March 2013, the NSA collected 3 billion pieces of data in the USA alone.[8]
- A court order ruled that Verizone has to provide to the NSA information on national and international phone calls on a daily basis.[9]

The details of the electronic surveillance operations are unknown. Those involved have continuously denied and downplayed these operations: Google's CEO Larry Page said that the NSA has no direct access to Google's servers.[10] Facebook's CEO Mark Zuckerberg,[11] Apple, Microsoft and Yahoo[12] made the same claim. AOL denied having any knowledge of the existence of PRISM.[13] Whom should one believe? Claims of Internet companies stand against leaked documents, in which the NSA says it has direct access to user data, and whistleblower Edward Snowden says that he was in the position to directly spy on every person whose email address he had.[14]

We should remember that Google in 2010 admitted in the Street View surveillance scandal that it had lied about the actual extent of surveillance.[15] It wrote: "we discovered that a statement made in a blog post on April 27 was incorrect. In that blog post, and in a technical note sent to data protection authorities the same day, we said that while Google did collect publicly broadcast SSID information (the WiFi network name) and MAC addresses (the unique number given to a device like a WiFi router) using Street View cars, we did not collect payload data (information sent over the network). But it's now clear that we have been mistakenly collecting samples of payload data from open (i.e. non-password-protected) WiFi networks, even though we never used that data in any Google products". Internet corporations earn money from personal data and as the Google example shows, they are not always keen on revealing the actual extent of surveillance. One therefore should not trust what private companies that collaborated with the NSA in spying on citizens say about their knowledge of PRISM. It is rather more feasible to assume that it is correct what the leaked documents and Snowden say, namely that the NSA has direct access to personal user data that large online corporations store.

Given the existence of PRISM, Occupy activists' fear that their activities are monitored by the police when using corporate social media are not illusionary, but representative of a dark reality. At the same time this surveillance system questions the very values of freedom of thought, speech and assembly that liberal ideology posits. In addition, it was revealed that the UK police monitored 9 000 activists, many of whom do not have a criminal record,[16] and that the British intelligence agency Government Communications Headquarters (GCHQ), as part of its project Tempora, monitors the world's phone and Internet traffic through access to fibre-optic cables.[17]

The concept of the military-industrial complex stresses the existence of collaborations in the security realm between private corporations and the state's institutions of internal and external defence. C. Wright Mills (1956, 7f) argued that there is a power elite that connects economic, political and military power: "There is no longer, on the one hand, an economy, and, on the other hand, a political order containing a military establishment unimportant to politics and to money-making. There is a political economy linked, in a thousand ways, with military institutions and decisions. ... there is an ever-increasing interlocking of economic, military, and political structures".

PRISM shows that the military-industrial complex contains a surveillance-industrial complex (Hayes 2009), into which social media are entangled: Facebook and Google both have more than

1 billion users and are probably the largest holders of personal data in the world. They and other private social media companies are first and foremost advertising companies that appropriate and commodify data on users' interests, communications, locations, online behaviour and social networks. They make profit out of data that users' online activities generate. They constantly monitor usage behaviour for this economic purpose. Since 9/11 there has been intensification and extension of surveillance that is based on the naïve technological-deterministic surveillance ideology that monitoring technologies, big data analysis and predictive algorithms can prevent terrorism. The reality of Woolwich, the South East London district where two suspected religious extremists killed a British soldier in May 2013, shows that terrorists can use low-tech tools such as machetes for targeted killings. High-tech surveillance will never be able to stop terrorism because most terrorists are smart enough not to announce their intentions on the Internet. It is precisely this surveillance ideology that has created intelligence agencies' interest in the big data held by social media corporations. Evidence[18] has shown that social media surveillance targets not just terrorists, but has also been directed at protestors and civil society activists. State institutions and private corporations have long collaborated in intelligence, but access to social media has taken the surveillance-industrial complex to a new dimension: it is now possible to obtain detailed access to a multitude of citizens' activities in converging social roles conducted in converging social spaces.

Yet the profits made by social media corporations are not the only economic dimension of the contemporary surveillance-industrial complex: The NSA has subcontracted and outsourced surveillance tasks to around 2000 private security companies[19] that make profits by spying on citizens. Booz Allen Hamilton, the private security company that Edward Snowden worked for until recently, is just one of these firms that follow the strategy of accumulation-by-surveillance. According to financial data[20], it had 24 500 employees in 2012 and its profits increased from US$ 25 million in 2010 to 84 million in 2011, 239 million in 2012 and 219 million in 2013. Surveillance is big business, both for online companies and those conducting the online spying for intelligence agencies.

The social media surveillance-industrial complex shows that a negative dialectic of enlightenment is at play in contemporary society: the military-industrial complex constantly undermines the very liberal values of the enlightenment, such as the freedoms of thought, speech, press and assembly as well as the security of the people's persons, houses, papers and effects. PRISM shows how in supposedly liberal democracies totalitarian forms of political-economic power negate enlightenment values. PRISM shows that Occupy activists who use Facebook or Google services can expect that all their revealed personal data is accessible to the police.

The OccupyMedia! Survey's respondents considered it likely that governments and corporate social media collaborate in monitoring activists. The data was collected 4-7 months before the existence of PRISM was revealed. The respondent stress that the corporate character of Facebook, Google, YouTube and Facebook interacts with state surveillance:

- "The other risk is that commercial sites might collaborate with government or corporate interests to close down sites if a threat to their interests became apparent" (#11).
- "Some social media are not only cooperating with authorities but proactively seeking out material to hand over to them, even when it has been known that this will lead to loss of life through torture. Of course I am thinking specifically of Facebook in cases known to occur during the

Tunisian and Egyptian revolutions at least" (#19).

- It is "often 'the 1%', rich people and institutions that own corporate networks, so there are the risks of monitoring, acquiescence to police, advanced tracking, and shut-down" (#170).

- "Yes, users of these platforms are agreeing to terms of service which may include the disclosure of their activities to law enforcement. Furthermore, closed platforms and software programs are inherently un-transparent" (#246).

Many survey respondents worried about the corporate character of Facebook, YouTube and Twitter, arguing that these platforms exploit users and monopolize social media:

- "We've tried to keep this as an entirely transparent and open movement, which I think is a good idea, because it would limit those risks. Facebook is generally exploitative, and controls the output of Facebook posts, the frequency they are seen by other people. It's a disaster and we shouldn't use it at all. But we still do" (#28).

- "Facebook = Tracebook. ... We're contributing to capitalism by putting our content for free" (#203).

- "Relying on an externally owned/operated platform is a risk, because it could be shutdown whenever. However, these are the best platforms (currently) for reaching the masses" (#205).

- "These platforms are involved in the power structure and at any time, can be used against movements and individuals. Having said that, there are few other options" (#283).

- "It is not appropriate to use the software technology of large corporations such as F**K and Twit, reddit, Tumblr, Meetup, etc. Through their creation of profit oriented walled gardens they are part of the problem and do not provide a solution" (#315).

- "YES. Google, Inc. has given Occupy Portland a very difficult time. Just take our Info email that after working for a good six months, decided to just stop working no matter how much attempts to restore it via Gmail! We ended up forwarding it to a Webmail account that was later phished, and so we currently use a riseup.net email account and dumped the corporate provider! ... Our servers have been attacked and malware corrupted our files; as it could have taken earlier if more communication were to occur, it is currently being fixed" (#403).

Many respondents stress that along with the corporate character of the dominant social media comes the risk of censorship and arbitrary shutdown. Some of them experienced that profiles, email addresses, pages or groups were shut down. In these cases it is unclear if the shutdown happened on purpose or as the result of an algorithm that automatically disables online resources if certain conditions are given (e.g. high level of activity, repeated sending of certain messages, anonymous profiles, use of pseudonyms, etc). No matter what the exact causes are, the effect is that political activists are limited in their capacity to communicate, which means that a private company denies them freedom of speech and expression. Some examples of censorship experiences:

- "Our HUGE 4000 person group was shutdown entirely and never resurfaced" (#49).
- "Massive Facebook censorship of certain topics and news articles (such as #S17). Have to be creative when posting in order to slip past the filters" (#67).
- "You have no idea how many Occupy sites on FB just recently got suspended or shutdown? Errrrrrrrrrrrrrrrrrr!!!" (#94).
- "the problem with using mainstream social media is the

countless times I've encountered censorship. Where services like Twitter or Facebook have deleted or suspended accounts or posts because they were Occupy content involving protest ... As a result, ... we failed to contact hundreds if not thousands of people attempting to spread a message across several networks" (#221).

- "Yes, if Facebook for example doesn't want certain things said on their website, they can/will remove them. Facebook, Twitter, Tumblr, etc. are corporations and naturally act in the interest of corporations and the capitalist ruling class that own them" (#222).
- "Censorship: Facebook continually interferes when I post stories on multiple Occupy Facebook pages, telling me that I might be a spammer or bot and shutting down my ability to multiple post for ten days to two weeks. Bastard" (#267).

Many respondents stress that it would be great to have viable alternatives to corporate social media, but that the problem is that Facebook, YouTube and Twitter are so dominant in terms of the number of users and therefore allow reaching the public to a better degree than alternative platforms such as Occupii, Diaspora* or N-1:

- "Of course, it's cooler to use non-commercial media, but there are benefits to using popular platforms because of the potential for reaching a wider network of people" (#11).
- "It is an issue for the movement that commercial platforms are the most used by those who we are trying to reach. There are new and experimental platforms because of Occupy, but they are not reaching the every one else (99%, if I'm forced to use that term) that we need to keep going" (#16).
- "It would be preferable if we would use only platforms under our control or under control of allies that were highly reliable and using only open source tools to do so,

but in order to reach the people who are not already involved we must use the platforms where these people are" (#19).

- "I think we should use non-commercial platforms" (#25).
- "You know you can be monitored when using the commercial platforms. You know for sure you are monitored by companies who want to sell you their stuff, but you cannot know whether or not you are followed by a government agency or whatever. But for me, that is meaningless. This 'risk' does not weigh up to the advantage you have using Facebook, because everyone uses it. If everyone was using Diaspora*, then I would have used Diaspora* to try to mobilize my friends and informing and keeping informed about protests and stuff" (#67).

Some respondents mentioned further problems, such as trolling (the deliberate disruption of communication on an online platform), communication problems and slacktivism (the substitution of street protest by online activities). Some examples:

- "We had a Facebook group, but whenever a new conversation was started, a few bad apples in a comment stream would kill the conversation. This led me to believe that political conversations and conversions would only take place in the physical public sphere, not the digital one" (#51).
- "The biggest risk is that it is too easy to miscommunicate and react poorly to others. There is something about being removed/not face-to-face that can inhibit the dialogue" (#56).
- "Risk of couch activism makes it so very hard to get people to actually go out in public and show support for the movement. They are fearful of what others will think of them" (#59).

- "Yes, it gives Internet activists (mainly Facebook) the idea of being very busy organising things, while people should do a lot more IRL [in real life]. It therefore supports apathy and disconnection sometimes. ... Events for protests that were created on Facebook, but not organised IRL. Many 'participants' in calls for protests on Facebook, but at least 70% of them doesn't show up at the actual demonstration. Protest twitter accounts that were blocked for obscure reasons during crucial moments of demonstrations (three times, different protests)" (#74).

- "Risks to be taken for granted and be turned into 'slacktivism', an activism without an actual movement" (#158).

5.5.2. Advantages of Corporate Social Media

The survey also used an open question for asking about advantages of commercial social media. The results are presented in Table 26. A minority (6.7%) sees no advantages. The biggest advantage that 69.5% of the respondents identify is that many users are on commercial social media, which allows reaching a broad public and everyday people who are not activists. Other important advantages that a significant share of respondents mentioned are that platforms such as Facebook and Twitter are relatively easy to use, allow fast and instantaneous communi-

Advantage	Frequency	Share (%)
High reach, reaching everyday people	196	69.5%
Easy to use	35	12.4%
Fast information and communication	31	11.0%
Global communication	8	2.8%
None	19	6.7%

Table 26: Identified advantages of Occupy's use of commercial social media, N=282

cation and publishing and enable communication at a global level.

The respondents relatively frequently use the following terms for indicating that tools such as Facebook and Twitter reach a lot of people: reach, broad outreach, spread, many people, public, everyday people, established, wide audience, popular, known by many, connected to mainstream population, breadth, more people, reaches the masses, exposure. Here are some example answers:

- "They [commercial social media] are generally easier to use and more people use the commercial platforms" (#10).
- "More people outside of the movement use commercial platforms so it's good for announcements and outreach. Sometimes commercial platforms seem more intuitive and easy to use" (#13).
- "These platforms are good outreach tools, unfortunately" (#16).
- "Reaching people that are not involved to begin with. Preaching to the choir doesn't do much at all" (#26).
- "More people use commercial Internet platforms. ... Occupii has not been useful because it is used by too few people" (#51).
- "All the activists are already there, but so are regular people. I think it's one of the main goals of the Occupy movement to reach out to the rest of the 99%. ... Facebook is the only place where we can speak to the people" (#63).
- "The only advantages are the volume of the voice, it's what most people use" (#109).
- "Gets to more people quicker using Facebook or alternatives because even friends or family who do not agree with the movement due to their own belief may have an a ha moment in one of the articles or pictures of our protest or gathering" (#138).

- "It does have a much larger user base, which allows for the information to be distributed to far more people than if a more niche site had been used" (#179).
- "Reach more unaware citizens" (#204).
- "It permits the Occupy message to get out to more people than just those actively involved in any Occupy work. We are having a problem engaging the public, so every little bit helps" (#211).
- "Yes – folks outside the choir use the commercial ones. That is how the movement grows, not being snotty and self-contained; though these alt-platforms definitely have a place; just not for beginners" (#262).
- "Spreading information to the people that are not aware of the non-commercial platforms" (#290).
- "All my friends/family not active in Occupy are able to see what Occupy is doing and remain informed" (#296).
- "The only advantage is that more people look at FB [Facebook] and the others than other platforms" (#312).
- "The only real advantage to using commercial internet platforms is that they tend to attract more viewers, which is important when one wishes to stage large-scale protests or disseminate information to as many people as possible" (#314).
- "To organize and create a movement you have to go to where the people are. We want everyone, we want to talk to them where they are comfortable" (#321).
- "Facebook has 1 billion users, making it the most incredible networking tool in history, even though it is a 'bad' company ... in a way, we are using the enemies tools to defeat the enemy" (#330).
- "Reaches the masses. Otherwise you are preaching to the choir" (#362).
- "All the big commercial ones have a strong user base. As much as we all hate Facebook, we all use it" (#408).   Here

are some answers that stress that social media enable fast and instantaneous communication:

- "As technology is so portable it was easier to get updates in realtime and communicate to a large group of people more efficiently" (#294).
- "Yes, it goes a lot faster!" (#300).
- "Yes, you can reach far more people in a quicker amount of time to announce protest dates, or provide live updates & streams" (#319).
- "So many more of the less active members of the 99% use these platforms than alternative sites, that these methods reached the wider 99% more quickly" (#345).
- "It can reach a mass amount of people and at a more rapid pace than bully pulpits and soap boxes" (#353).
- "Yes, provides a rapid, potentially world wide network to provide information about the movement" (#367).
- "The message is spread rapidly" (#417). Some users also stress that commercial social media are relatively easy to use. Some examples:
- "Ease of use, already prevalent mode of communication that Occupy can piggy-back on" (#88).
- "It is possible to reach many more people using these more popular, commercial forums. They're easy to use and a good way to spread more information quicker and further" (#222).
- "More ease at reaching more people" (#234).
- "More people use the commercial Internet platforms mentioned above therefore outreach can be easier" (#243).
- "Never in my lifetime has the news of international unrests been shared so effectively and immediately as they have in the past year" (#258).
- "Accessible, convenient to use with all social interaction" (#318).
- "Easy to maintain and use" (#403).

5.5.3. Advantages of Alternative Social Media

One open question in the survey asked respondents about advantages of non-commercial social media such as Diaspora*, N-1, Occupii, InterOccupy teleconferences, OccupyTalk voice chat, etc. The most important results are shown in Table 27.

Advantage	Frequency	Share (%)
Don't know	94	34.1%
Privacy, less surveillance, less censorship	73	26.4%
Non-profit, non-commercial	43	15.6%
Communication and coordination inside the movement	42	15.2%
None	38	13.8%

Table 27: Identified advantages of Occupy's use of non-commercial social media, N=276

There is a relatively large share of respondents who are unfamiliar with alternative social media (34.1%), indicate this circumstance and therefore say that they don't know how to answer. About half of the respondents identify specific advantages of alternative social media: 26.4% of the respondents say that these platforms are more privacy-friendly than commercial ones because they are run by activists and are therefore more unlikely to be censored or controlled by the police. Whereas commercial platforms are predominantly perceived as having large reach, but a high risk of surveillance and censorship, alternative platforms are valued for enabling a reduction of these risks. 15.6% stress that the non-profit and non-commercial character of alternative social media is important and fits the Occupy movement's goals. 15.2% highlight that alternative social media are a good tool for internal communication and coordination inside of the Occupy movement.

Here are examples of typical answers of those who say they do not know how to comment and have no experience with alternative social media:

- "Not sure. I should look into these more" (#56).
- "I'm not sure. I have never used them" (#76).
- "I honestly haven't used them so can't answer this question. I spend about 8 hours a day on FB and Twitter and that seems to work pretty well" (#93).
- "No opinion since I have never used them" (#135).
- "I don't have experience with the non commercial platforms" (#256).

Here are some examples for arguments that stress that activists' privacy is larger on non-commercial platforms and that on these social media there is less risk of police surveillance and censorship:

- "More privacy control" (#8).
- "They provide a safer place to communicate amongst ourselves without being vulnerable to trolls" (#16).
- "The primary advantage is the lack of censorship in terms of political message" (#38).
- "Yes, many of us used N-1 because it's safer" (#155).
- "We own them, and so risks about monitoring etc. are diminished" (#170).
- "Lessened chance of state surveillance" (#210).
- "More privacy less censorship" (#259).
- "Yes, greater privacy" (#295).
- "Yes, less chance of government spying" (#367)

A significant share of respondents argues that they find it an

advantage that alternative platforms such as Occupii, Diaspora*
and N-1 are non-commercial, non-profit and therefore do not
exploit users. These platforms would fit the logic of the Occupy
movement that is critical of capitalism. The respondents argue
that protest communication should not benefit corporations
because the Occupy movement is critical of corporations. Some
example answers:

- "[On these platforms] protesting does not make money for
  somebody else" (#8).
- "Possibly more secure, almost certainly more ethical in that
  they're probably not putting money into the pockets of the
  1%" (#13).
- "demonstrates that there are alternatives, helps to develop
  better tools for movements, challenges the corporates"
  (#109).
- "They are secure, they are not full of ads and they have
  clearer parameters and more sophisticated tools" (#113)
- "It is great to be focused and advertisement free. Also to
  have a network of like-minded individuals working
  together within a worldwide networked system. All great
  tools!" (#123).
- "Yes, distributed, non-proprietary, free (freedom) (really
  democratic) tools" (#191).
- "Owned and managed by us, more control of our content"
  (#413).

Here are examples for responses that stress the importance of
alternative social media as tools of movement-internal communication for discussions and coordination:

- "the advantages are that many individuals using the
  spaces share your political interests and your information
  will not be sold to advertisers" (#239).
- "sharing with like-minded people" (#255).

- "Platforms that are better tailored for the kinds of communications we need can do better than those designed for more general socializing" (#269).
- "allows for deep conversations and for affinity groups to meet and chat" (#281).
- "it is more about internal communications so yes, it is good for internal communications to get off the structures that you are trying to bring down" (#321).
- "Only to communicate within the movement. Otherwise it's like preaching to the choir" (#333).
- "Yes, these platforms are great for internal communication but not for outreach" (#342).

5.5.4. Disadvantages of Alternative Social Media

One survey question asked about perceived disadvantages of alternative social media. The results are shown in Table 28.

Disadvantage	Frequency	Share (%)
Low reach	84	30.7%
None	75	27.3%
Resource-intensive	52	19.0%
Don't know	48	17.5%
Lack of technological quality	9	3.3%

Table 28: Identified disadvantages of Occupy's use of non-commercial social media, N=274

17.5% of the respondents say they lack experience with alternative social media and therefore do not know how to answer. 27.3% say the there are no disadvantages if the Occupy movement uses alternative social media. 30.7% argue that alternative social media only have a low reach and do not allow reaching out to the general public. These respondents fear that by using alternative social media, the Occupy movement isolates itself, does not speak to the public and preaches to the choir. 19.0% mentioned that operating and using these platforms requires that the movement mobilizes a lot of resources: time, money, donations, workforce, software development and maintenance skills, servers, computers, webspace.

Here are some examples for arguments employed by respondents who say that alternative social media have a low reach:

- "Only those already interested are using them - leaving out the rest of the world" (#2).
- "Lack of outreach if we stuck purely to this. Inaccessibility to non-geeks sometimes" (#13).
- "I think there's a danger of being isolated and only being around people who share your own views" (#28).
- "Yes, it makes the movement appear cultish and secretive" (#37).
- "Only tech-savvy users use alternative platforms. Those who haven't adopted the technology (i.e. the general public) are excluded from important conversations" (#51).
- "Many are too small to make a difference" (#67).
- "It absorbs competent volunteer effort (which is always in very short supply), and risks isolating the movement in its own echo chamber, rather than having it constantly reach out and raise awareness that people who are unhappy with the status quo are not alone" (#82).
- "Closed systems offer security, but also limit access" (#129).
- "They can separate the struggle from average, politically inactive/ I'll informed people. Less people see the content" (#223).
- "Only that people may be unaware of them – like me! – even though they are part of the movement" (#263).

- "Reduces potential of spread of movement as items cannot be shared with non-members potentially interested in engagement" (#325).
- "I've never heard of most of them" (#408).
- "Even grandma has Facebook and while Facebook has effectively subverted movements since Occupy's inception it's notoriety and easy search option for people of all walks is an advantage. People have to know these places exist otherwise we're preaching to the choir" (#429).

Respondents argue that operating, using and maintaining alternative social media requires a large amount of different resources:

- "The maintenance of such platforms might take lots of time from the people working with it" (#20).
- "Developing software is hard" (#23).
- "It does take a lot of time and energy for the people that do the development and maintenance" (#39).
- "Someone has to pay for them" (#41).
- "Maintenance, people dedicating hours and skills towards upkeep, mass communications tools depending on very few people to keep running them" (#69).
- "Yes, it is an awful lot of energy poured into infrastructure that ultimately appears to compete with itself, rather than creating a larger force of numbers and influence in already existing platforms (virtual spaces). ... alternative platforms that seem to suck up time, energy and resources, and are ultimately less convenient to use because they are SO SPECIFIC to the movement" (#113).
- "You need a connection, wifi access etc. data needs backing up and sites need admin, it does take significant hours" (#157).
- "The massive time commitment and the fact most people

won't, and will never, use them" (#170).

- "Workload of those who develop and/or manage these custom platforms" (#176).
- "The finances may not be sufficient to support maintenance" (#228).
- "Financially it is problematic since Occupy has no internalized economy, yet. Finding the people power, required to generate and keep sites going, could also be problematic; especially since they would more likely than not be volunteers" (#251).
- "Learning curve, especially for things that are excessively techy" (#262).
- "There is an overhead in building our own, but we will learn a lot in the process, and more of us need to be involved in the whole process of improving our communications and community building" (#269).
- "Well, hosting these can get expensive, and you are not guaranteed donations, which might pose a problem" (#329).
- "I assume it takes resources and time away from doing other things and requires people with certain technical expertise" (#339).
- "Yes in the sense that it requires constant programming, it may not be as visible to newcomers and sometimes they weren't maintained (when the key people got arrested)" (#360).
- "It requires time and man-power" (#364).

6. Interpreting the Data: Social Movement Media in Crisis Capitalism

6.1. Defining the Occupy Movement

An important task of the survey was to analyse how Occupy activists define the movement and what kind of movement it is for them (research question 1).

Occupy has, like every social movement, opponents, goals, methods of protest and organizational structures (Fuchs 2006).

Occupy *opposes* capitalism's problems, injustice, inequality, unfairness, austerity measures, financial and governmental corruption, a police state, the centralization of political power, war, violence, racism and homophobia. The identified *goals* of the Occupy movement are alternatives to capitalism, participatory democracy; a just, fair and equitable society; a sustainable society, a better world, the abolition of the influence of the economy on politics; making corporations, governments and banks accountable for their actions; autonomy, freedom and self-determination, raising political awareness and creating a peaceful society.

Occupy's *methods of protest* include occupations of public spaces for reclaiming such spaces and the public sphere, non-violence, humor and glamor.

Respondents see Occupy *organized* in such a way that it is a grassroots movement that is networked, diverse, global, tries to establish new ways of life, is based on mutual aid, gives hope that change is possible and gives people a voice in political engagement.

The empirical results overall confirm the assumption of political theorists that Occupy is a movement that struggles to reclaim the commons of society that are produced by all, but have under neoliberal capitalism been increasingly privatized and commodified. Hardt and Negri (2012, Opening) argue that

Occupy movements are "struggles for the common, then, in the sense that they contest the injustices of neoliberalism and, ultimately, the rule of private property". Slavoj Žižek (2012, 83) writes that Occupy activists "care about the commons – the commons of nature, of knowledge – which are threatened by the system". The Occupy movement would be discontent with "capitalism as a system" and with the reduction of democracy to representation (Žižek 2012, 87). For Alain Badiou (2012, 111), Occupy stands for the "creation in common of the collective destiny". For Jodi Dean (2012, 178), Occupy advances "a new assertion of the common and commons". David Harvey (2012, 25) sees Occupy as urban social movement that reclaims "their right to the city – their right to change the world, to change life, and to reinvent the city more after their hearts' desire" and the right to urban commons that were created by collective labour" (Harvey 2012, 78).

The global justice movement that emerged with the "battle of Seattle" in 1999 was a first indication of the return of class politics. What mainly differed in comparison to Occupy was the societal context: there was no global economic crisis. The crisis that started in 2008 marks a big rupture. It suddenly became evident through economic reality that capitalism is a crisis-ridden system and that neoliberalism fosters massive socio-economic inequality. The global justice movement constantly warned about the consequences of financialization and neoliber-alism, but before the crisis started those in power could more easily downplay or ignore these warnings. In 2008, the contradic-tions of contemporary capitalism exploded in a global crisis. The warnings can now no longer be disregarded because they have become an economic reality that manifests itself in bankruptcy, debt, unemployment, evictions, food crises, misery, austerity – and protests.

But not only context, but also strategy discerns Occupy from the global justice movement: Whereas the latter followed mainly the strategy of trying to block events where the global political-economic elite met and took decisions that affected the lives of people globally, in combination with organizing counter-summits such as the World Social Forum or the European Social Forum, Occupy does not move flexibly in space, but occupies and encamps places. The global justice movement's occupations were temporary (there was a planned beginning and a planned end) and took the form of demonstrations in certain places, where the powerful met, so space was appropriated in a temporally limited manner and in a spatially flexible way, depending on where the powerful were meeting. In contrast, a strategy of the Occupy movements, not only in the USA and Europe, but also in the Arab spring and other parts of the world, was to claim strategic urban places (such as Tahrir Square in Cairo, Syntagma Square in Athens, Puerta del Sol in Madrid, Plaça Catalunya in Barcelona, Zuccotti Park in New York or Taksim Square in Istanbul) as common property of the movement, where protest practices happen for an undefined period of time. Whereas the global justice movement was placeless and dynamically located in global space, Occupy is a place-based movement.

David Harvey (2012) points out this circumstance by characterizing Occupy as urban movement. The assembly of a large number of people in squares and the organization of these squares as political places controlled by activists is a threat to those in power. It makes visible the discontentment of people in a central spatial environment. The claim to urban space as a common also reflects citizens' dissatisfaction with capitalism's exploitation and destruction of commons such as housing, social security, communication, culture, nature, education, health care and human survival. Reclaiming space is at the same time the symbol for the political demand to reclaim all of society from the control exerted by capital.

But the control of spaces and the reclaiming of certain urban spaces as common property of the people is not the only strategy of resistance, the control of time is also a threat to those in power: whereas a demonstration or campaign is planned for a limited time, the encampments and occupations do not plan on a temporal limit, but make the political claim that spaces are liberated and that this liberation has started and will never stop. Of course there are different temporal outcomes of such urban rebellions: whereas Occupy Wall Street was dissolved by police violence, which put an artificial temporal end point to the occupation, the struggles in Egypt and Tunisia turned into successful revolutions that occupied time in another sense: they put an end to old regimes and opened up space and time for new political opportunities.

Whereas Manuel Castells (1996) described contemporary society as moving from the logic of the space of places to the logic of the space of flows that is characterized by timeless time and placeless space so that contemporary movements are timeless and placeless movements (Castells 1997), the Occupy movement makes clear that the space of flows was primarily the space of capital and that the logic of common places can be a global and networked logic of resistance. It grounds resistances in places, so it is not placeless, but uses places as a form of power. It understands timelessness not primarily as the overcoming of temporal distance in globalization processes, but as the claim that the revolution/rebellion has started and will not stop until those in power are gone and new economic and political times can begin. Occupy is the attempt to open up time, to make time historical in the process of revolution.

6.2. Occupy and Social Media

The survey also aimed at finding out how activists perceive the role of social media in their protests. This task was formulated in research question 2: What is activists' perceived role of social media in the Occupy movement?

Four common positions on the role of social media in the Occupy movement can be identified. These four positions represent four logical possibilities of connecting technology and society: technology as the determining factor, society as the determining factor, two independent factors, mutual and contradictory relationship.

Techno-deterministic views of the role of media in protests hold that media are causes of protests. Castells says that the Occupy movement "was born on the Internet, diffused by the Internet, and maintained its presence on the Internet" and that its "material form of existence was the *occupation of public space*" (Castells 2012, 168). Social "networks on the Internet allowed the experience to be communicated and amplified, bringing the entire world into the movement" (Castells 2012, 169). Like Castells, his former PhD student Jeffrey Juris (2012) assumes that social media "generate" protests.

Social constructivism argues that we have been witnessing social rebellions and social revolutions, where social media have had minor importance. Social media would be no relevant factor in rebellions. Such accounts typically talk about different political aspects of the movement, but ignore the dimension of the media (e.g. Chomsky 2012).

Dualism argues that social media are important tools of social movements and that contemporary revolutions and protests are both social and technological revolutions. For the journalist Paul Mason, the new rebellions, including the Occupy movement, have been "caused by the near collapse of free-market capitalism combined with an upswing in technical innovation, a surge in desire for individual freedom and a change in human consciousness about what freedom means" (Mason 2012, 3).

The majority of the respondents in the OccupyMedia! Survey do not share techno-deterministic, constructivist and dualist positions, but have a dialectical view of the role of social media in protests, stressing the antagonistic character of social media as having contradictory positive and negative potentials as tools of control/domination and struggles. They point out social media's opportunities for supporting protest movements' networking, mobilization and potential to bypass the mainstream media. Simultaneously they stress that there are dangers such as surveillance, censorship, separation from street protests, infiltration by the police and secret services, corporate control and a stratified visibility and attention economy. These risks would be especially present on the dominant commercial platforms such as Facebook and Twitter. Some activists therefore point out the need for Occupy to create and control its own social media, which would face resource limits and the fact that many people are scared to leave corporate social media because they have many contacts there.

The insights of the OccupyMedia! Survey about the dialectical role of social media can be generalized in the form of a model that shows the dialectic of protests and the media (see figure 4).

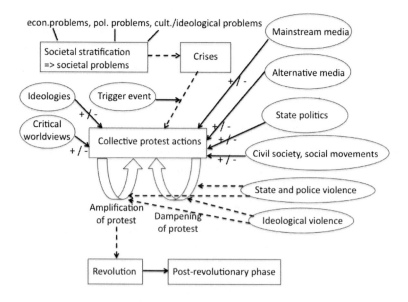

Figure 4: A model of protests and the role of crises, the media, ideology and politics

Protests have an objective foundation that is grounded in the contradictions of society, i.e. forms of domination that cause problems that are economic, political and cultural in nature. Societal problems can result in (economic, political, cultural/ideological) crises[21] if they are temporally persistent and cannot be easily overcome. Crises do not automatically result in protests, but are an objective and necessary, although not sufficient condition of protest. If crisis dimensions converge and interact, then we can speak of a societal crisis. Protests require a substantial recognition within public perception that there are societal problems, that these problems are unbearable and a scandal and that something needs to be changed. Often actual protests and movements are triggered and continuously intensified by certain events (such as the arrest of Rosa Parks in the US civil rights movement, the public suicide of Mohamed Bouazizi in the 2011 Tunisian revolution, the killing of Khaled Mohamed Saeed by the police in the 2011 Egyptian revolution, the pepper-spraying of activists by NYPD officer Anthony Bologna and the mass arrest of Occupy Wall Street activists on Brooklyn Bridge, the massive violence of Turkish police forces against protestors occupying Istanbul's Taksim Square etc).

It is precisely here that Castells' (2012) focus on the emotions of outrage and hope plays a role in the potential transition from crises to protests. Subjective perceptions and emotions are, however, not the only factor because they are conditioned and influenced by politics, the media and culture/ideology. The way state politics, mainstream media and ideology, on the one hand, and oppositional politics/social movements, alternative media and alternative worldviews on the other, connect to human subjects, directly influences the conditions of protests. They can have rather amplifying, rather neutral or rather dampening effects on protests. So for example racist media coverage can advance racist stereotypes and/or the insight that the media and contemporary society are racist in-themselves. The media –

social media, the Internet and all other media – are contradictory because we live in a society of contradictions. As a consequence, their effects are actually contradictory, they can dampen/forestall or amplify/advance protest or have not much effect at all.

Also, different media (e.g. alternative media and commercial media) stand in a contradictory relation with each other that can result in a power struggle. And the media are not the only factors that influence the conditions of protest – they also stand in contradictory relations with politics and ideology/culture that also influence the conditions of protest. So whether protest emerges or not is shaped by multiple factors that are so complex that it cannot be calculated or forecast if protest will emerge as result of a certain crisis or not. Once protests have emerged, media, politics and culture continue to have permanent contradictory influences on them and it is undetermined if these factors have rather neutral, amplifying or dampening effects on protest. Protests in antagonistic societies often call forth policing and police action, so the state reacts to social movements with its organized form of violence. State violence against protests and ideological violence against movements (in the forms of delegitimizing attacks by the media, politicians and others) can again have amplifying, dampening or insignificant effects on protests.

If there is a protest amplification spiral, protest may grow to larger and larger dimensions, which can eventually, but not necessarily, result in a revolution – a breakdown and fundamental reconstitution/renewal of the economy, politics and worldviews caused by an overthrow of society by a social movement that puts the revolutionary forces into power and control of the major economic, political and moral structures (see Goodwin 2001, 9). Every revolution results in a post-revolutionary phase, in which the reconstruction and renewal of society begins, and here the legacy of conflict and the remnants or memory of the old society can pose challenges.

Social media in a contradictory society (made up of class conflicts and other conflicts between dominant and dominated groups) are likely to have a contradictory character: they do not necessarily and automatically support/amplify or dampen/limit rebellions, but rather pose contradictory potentials that stand in contradictions with influences by the state, ideology and capitalism.

6.3. Communicating Activism

One task of the research focused on analysing how Occupy activists communicate in protest practices. It was expressed in research question 3: How often do Occupy activists use certain media and communication forms?

Research question 3 was subdivided into four further questions: 3.1. How often do Occupy activists use certain media and communication forms for informing themselves about protests and occupations? 3.2. How often do Occupy activists create content for or about the movement with the help of certain media? 3.3. How often do Occupy activists use certain media and communication forms for communication with other activists? 3.4. How often do Occupy activists use certain media and communication forms for trying to mobilize people for protests and occupations?

Personal face-to-face conversations are the most important source of information about the Occupy movement. Traditional media do not play a major role, rather Occupy websites, personal emails, email mailing lists, Twitter and YouTube are other important sources of information. Commercial online media are more heavily used for obtaining information, sharing user-generated content and protest mobilization communication than non-commercial platforms such as Occupii, N-1 and Diaspora*.

Only a minority of activists frequently create and share user-generated content. Around half of all respondents conducted simpler task such as posting a picture on a social networking site at least once a month, whereas 30% uploaded a video to YouTube. It seems to be a smaller group of activists of around 10-20% of the activists that specializes in social media activism and makes use of technologies such as video live feeds, social networking sites, blogs, video sharing and alternative news services.

The personal conversation is the most frequent form of communication in the Occupy movement, followed by communication on Facebook, email, mailing lists and Twitter.   Activists use multiple media for mobilization-oriented communication: The data indicates that face-to-face communication, Facebook, email, phone, SMS and Twitter are the most important media that Occupy activists employ for trying to mobilize others for protests.

The frequency of activism tends to positively influence the frequency of media use for informing oneself about the movement, sharing user-generated content online, communication between activists using various media and using media for protest mobilization communication. The use of face-to-face communication and online communication tend to mutually reinforce each other. The use of various online media for information, the sharing of user-generated content and protest mobilization also tends to mutually reinforce each other.

6.4. Corporate and Alternative Social Media

Activists say that the largest risk of commercial social media is the surveillance of communication. They are especially critical and at the same time highly aware of the police's monitoring of activists' online communication and activities. The existence of the PRISM surveillance system has validated that these fears and reflects actual reality of large-scale surveillance of the Internet by UK and US government institutions. The respondents tend to be worried about the corporate character of social media platforms, stress that Facebook, Twitter and YouTube monopolize social media, exploit users and that along with these platforms' character comes the risk of deliberate and algorithmic censorship, which limits activists' freedom of speech and expression. Quite a few respondents indicate that they experienced online censorship or police surveillance themselves. The major advantage of commercial social media that the respondents identify is that they have many users, which potentially enables the Occupy movement to reach a broad public with its political ideas. They further stress that platforms such as Facebook and Twitter are relatively easy to use, allow fast and instantaneous communication and publishing and enable communication at a global level.

Corporate social media are shaped by an ambivalent dialectic: On the one hand they provide activists the potential to reach out to a broad public, but on the other hand the more the activists rely on these platforms for organizing their public and private communication, the more vulnerable to police surveillance and censorship they become.

There are also alternative social media platforms such as Occupii, N-1 and Diaspora*. 34.1% of the respondents say they cannot answer what advantages there are for alternative social media. Those who answered the question argue that alternative platforms are more privacy-friendly than commercial ones because they are run by activists and are therefore more unlikely to be censored or controlled by the police. Further advantages named are the non-profit and non-commercial character of alternative social media and their suitability as tools for the movement's internal communication and coordination. Whereas commercial platforms are predominantly perceived as having large reach, but a high risk of surveillance and censorship, alternative platforms are valued for the minimization of these risks. Alternative non-profit, non-commercial social media are also shaped by an ambivalent dialectic: On the one hand Occupy activists like these platform's organization model and say that it fits the movement's criticism of corporations and exploitation, and they also reduce the risk of censorship and police surveillance, but on the other hand the small user base of these platforms poses the problem that they cannot be used for reaching the broader public of non-activists, and the non-profit nature of these platforms makes it difficult to organize the resources (time, money, workforce, webspace, programming skills, etc) that a movement needs for running, controlling, maintaining and continuously updating its own social media. The movement-run social networking site occupii.org explains that its operating costs were first covered by administrators and some members, but that maintaining the platform requires more contributions:

> "The monthly payments to keep Occupii.org going have, for the last year, been sourced from the administrators and contributions from some members. This support is much appreciated and can not be celebrated enough.
>
> Occupii.org is an advert free zone. In order to keep this space free of corporate sponsors and/or adverts, we need to draw attention to the on-going costs of keeping this site available and ask for your help where, if and when possible.
>
> In requesting this support from the community we also want to be clear that no member need feel that they are being asked to give what they don't have, or that they will be thought of as less valuable because they are unable to help out with the maintenance costs.
>
> The monthly amount is £40. If 20 of us donated £2 a month for example, it would be covered. Please donate/help if you can. No amount is too small" (http://occupii.org/, accessed on April 28, 2013).

The statement shows the advantages of being non-profit (no corporate influence, the movement is in control of the platform) as well as the problem of mobilizing resources for alternative media.

Many respondents stress that it is good and an advantage to use alternative, non-commercial platforms, but that the problem is that these platforms do not have a large amount of users so that using the dominant corporate social media is the only way for reaching out to the public. Corporate social media on the one hand give access to a large public and at the same time have high risks of censorship and surveillance. There is a disquieting negative dialectic of public visibility on the one side and control on the other side that activists are confronted with when using corporate social media for political communication.

Examples of the censorship risks on Facebook could be found during the Egyptian revolution. Facebook blocked the group "My name is Khaled Mohamed Said", arguing that copyrights were infringed on it (Ghonim 2012, 113). Also the Facebook group "We are all Khaled Said" that was managed by social media activist Wael Ghonim was blocked (Ghonim 2012, 117). After an inquiry by the admin, Facebook answered that fake accounts had been used for administering the group (Ghonim 2012, 118). After public and media pressure, the group went up again after 24 hours. In this example, Facebook's argument that a political Facebook group that is involved in organizing protests in a country, where the opposition is tortured and killed, shall not be operated by fake accounts, but only by real name ones, is particularly striking and odd because it completely ignores the fear of activists, who risks their lives, to be discovered, tortured or even killed and the resulting need to stay anonymous.

There is also the risk of police control and monitoring on commercial social media, as evidenced by the existence of the PRISM surveillance system. In September 2012, Twitter followed a court order and handed over data about Malcolm Harris' Twitter use (email address, postings, etc). Harris was charged for disorderly conduct and arrested at an Occupy protest that took place on Brooklyn Bridge in 2011. "Prosecutors say that messages posted by Harris – who goes by the twitter handle @destructuremal – could show whether the defendant was aware that he was breaking police orders relating to the demo" (*The Guardian Online*, Twitter complies with prosecutors to surrender Occupy activist's tweets. September 14th, 2012).

Queen's Counsel John Cooper warns in this context that the police aims at monitoring activists' social media use: "The police are aware and are getting more aware of powers to force and compel platforms to reveal anonymous sites. … activists are putting themselves at more risk. Police will be following key Twitter sites, not only those of the activists but also other interesting figures. They know how to use them to keep up with rioting and to find alleged rioters. … In the same way they used to monitor mobile phones when they were trying to police impromptu raves, they are doing the same with Twitter and Facebook, as those who say too much on social media will find" (*The Independent Online*, Activists warned to watch what they say as social media monitoring becomes next big thing in law enforcement. October 1st, 2012). "Prosecutors say the tweets, which are no longer available online, may demonstrate that Harris knew police had told protesters not to walk on the roadway" (*The Huffington Post*, Twitter must produce Occupy protester Malcolm Harris' tweet or face contempt. November 9th, 2011).

Handing over user data to the police is regulated in both Twitter's and Facebook's terms of use: "we may preserve or disclose your information if we believe that it is reasonably necessary to comply with a law, regulation or legal request" (Twitter Privacy Policy, version from May 17th, 2012). "We may access, preserve and share your information in response to a legal request (like a search warrant, court order or subpoena) if we have a good faith belief that the law requires us to do so. … We may also access, preserve and share information when we have a good faith belief it is necessary to: detect, prevent and address fraud and other illegal activity; to protect ourselves, you and others, including as part of investigations; and to prevent death or imminent bodily harm" (Facebook Data Use Policy, version from December 11th, 2012). Activist-controlled platforms have less criminalization risk because they do not lack the distance from activism that the makers of Facebook and Twitter have. Given that Twitter and Facebook are large corporations themselves, one cannot assume that they do not see Occupy as dangerous and that they have an immanent interest in protecting activists' freedoms.

Non-commercial social media are embedded into an antagonism characteristic for alternative media (see Sandoval and Fuchs 2010, Fuchs 2010): they publish and mostly do not censor critical voices, but are often confronted with a lack of resources and visibility. Given the existence of the PRISM surveillance system, in which the major social media platforms Facebook and Google actively participate, Occupy activists must assume to be monitored by the police when using these platforms. Alternative platforms therefore become a crucial domain for avoiding being monitored and trying to obtain freedom of speech, assembly and thought that should be guaranteed by liberal states that nonetheless violate this fundamental right through their surveillance practices.

Alternative media in capitalism are facing structural inequality: Corporate media centralize resources, users, audiences, attention and markets because capital investments and monetary profits allow them to generate these resources. Alternative media have a different model. They often do not want to be commercial because they are critical of capitalism and thereby face the problem of how to mobilize resources in a capitalist world, where the main enabling factors of resource control are money and commodity logic.

The conducted study shows that Occupy activists see large positive potentials of alternative social media, but are at the same time aware of and worried about the lack of visibility and these platforms' small user base as well as the problem of how to mobilize resources for operating such online media as self-organized, non-commercial, non-profit movement-controlled projects that reject the logic of advertising, commodification and capital accumulation.

The problem that the monopoly power of Facebook, Twitter, YouTube and similar corporate platforms poses for alternative social media becomes evident if one looks at usage data: In the 3 month period between January 19th and April 19th, 2013, Facebook was the second most accessed web platform in the world with an access rate of 43.41% of all Internet users. YouTube was ranked third (33.6%) and Twitter 12th (6.8%).[22] This means that in this three-month period Facebook had on average 1 billion users, YouTube 800 million and Twitter 160 million. In contrast, Diaspora* was with a reach of 0.00213% of the world's Internet users in the same period was ranked in position 77 239 in the list of the most accessed websites in the world, N-1 held position 287 730 (reach: 0.00050%) and Occupii rank 2 840 391 (reach: 0.000040%). This means that Diaspora* had in the three-month period of analysis on average 50 000 active users, N-1 12 000 and Occupii 1000. There are inequalities of money, reputation, users, visibility and resources in general that are caused by capitalism and that shape the realities of alternative media and therefore also of alternative social media.

Jürgen Habermas's concept of the public sphere is a notion that on the one hand describes an ideal political world, in which everyone's political voice is heard and has an influence. But importantly the concept is also a notion of critique that denounces the limits of the public sphere in bourgeois society that proclaims liberal values such as the freedoms of speech, opinion, expression, association and assembly and at the same time immanently violates these values by structural inequalities. Liberal ideology postulates individual freedoms (of speech, opinion, association, assembly) as universal rights, but the particularistic and stratified class character of capitalism undermines these universal rights and creates inequality and therefore unequal access to the public sphere.

There are specifically two immanent limits of the bourgeois public sphere that Habermas discusses:

- The limitation of freedom of speech and public opinion: individuals do not always have the same formal education and material resources for participating in public sphere (Habermas 1989, 227).
- The limitation of freedom of association and assembly: big political and economic organisations "enjoy an oligopoly of the publicistically effective and politically relevant formation of assemblies and associations" (Habermas 1989, 228).

The bourgeois public sphere creates its own limits and thereby its own immanent critique. The relationship of alternative and mainstream social media is shaped by these two limits of the bourgeois public sphere:

- Alternative social media tend to have much less resources (programmers, work time, money, users, reputation, hardware, server space, bandwidth, etc) than corporate social media.
- The dominant corporate social media (Facebook, YouTube, Twitter, LinkedIn, Weibo, etc) enjoy an oligopoly of visibility and attention that disadvantages alternative non-commercial platforms.

The accumulation of money, decision-power and reputation that is characteristic of capitalist society in general privileges big organizations. In the social media world, it creates inequalities between corporate and non-corporate platform operators. The Occupy movement and other protest movements are embedded into the antagonism between corporate and non-corporate media. They want to reach out to the public and communicate their political visions, goals and ideas to as many people as possible. Occupy is critical of corporations and therefore shares with alternative social media the logic of the negation of capitalism. It stands in contradiction with the logic of commerce, advertising and capital accumulation that shapes corporate social media, yet this very logic creates monopoly structures that attract many users to the dominant platforms, which makes using these media for Occupy on the one hand attractive, but on the other hand highly risky. The movement opposes the 1%, yet the means of communication are owned by parts of the 1%. Alternative means of communication are available, but organizing them is resource-intensive under conditions of capitalist-induced resource precarity that discriminates social movements and privileges corporations. These alternative means also face a capitalist attention economy, in which usage, visibility and presence tends to be monopolized by capitalist organizations. Alternative media pose advantages, yet are difficult to organize in a capitalist society. The tendency of their resource and visibility precariousness shows the totalitarian character of capitalism that limits the freedom of speech, opinion, association and assembly of social movements and alternative media.

7. Alternatives

So the question arises: what can be done in order to foster alternative social media that support protest movements? The survey included one question that offered some organization models and asked the respondents which one they thought would be the best one for alternative social media. It asked: "As you may know, commercial social media platforms (such as YouTube, Facebook, Twitter, etc) fund their operations and make profit by the use of a business model that is based on targeted advertising and the monitoring and selling of user data. Social movement media that are not controlled by companies, but by a movement like Occupy, need certain resources (work time, editors, hardware, software, reporters, etc) for their operation. What do you think is the best way for organising the necessary resources in order to run an alternative online service like Occupii or TheGlobal Square?" There were six different answer options (for-profit with targeted advertising, state funding, donations, usage fees non-profit, usage fees for-profit, other). Around one fourth of the respondents selected the option "other" and specified this choice. I analysed the answers and partly recoded

Model	Frequency	Share (%)
For-profit, targeted advertising	23	8.0%
State funding	20	7.0%
Voluntary donations	157	54.7%
Usage fees, non-profit	27	9.4%
Usage fees, for-profit	2	0.7%
Other	45	15.7%
I do not know	13	4.5%

Table 29: Respondents' view on the best model for obtaining resources in order to run alternative online media, N=287

them. Some answers corresponded to some of the other options and were therefore recoded. I also introduced a new code for answers, in which the respondents said that they are unsure or do not know. Table 29 shows the results.

More than half of the respondents (54.7%) favour voluntary donations, which is by far the most popular resource model. 9.4% prefer the introduction of usage fees if the platform is non-profit, 8.7% favour for-profit models (usage fees for profit: 0.7%, targeted advertising for profit: 8.0%). 7.0% opted for state funding as favourite resource model. 15.7% suggested other models, such as for example voluntary work without wages and budget, the combination of donations and advertising, the combination of donations and state funding, the combination of donations and fees, voluntary donation of work time instead of money, the use of open source software, the combination of all elements, selective advertising, a free basic and a paid premium service and the suggestion that Occupy should develop a new mainstream social medium.

The survey asked those respondents, who indicated that they favour a donation model for alternative social media, how much money they would be willing to donate per month for such projects. Table 30 presents the results.

Currency	N	Min.	Max.	Median	Mean
€	18	0	30	9.0	9.7
US$	93	0	100	10.0	11.6
£	24	0	50	5.0	7.0

Table 30: Amount that respondents who favour donation-models for alternative social media are willing to donate per month

The mean value that respondents who favour donation-based models of alternative social media are willing to donate per month to alternative social media is around 10 €. This sum is comparable to what a lot of people spend per month on their telephone bill or the licence fee for public broadcasting.

All of these models can have potential problems: Donations are voluntary. It can be difficult to mobilize supporters, the risk that only a small number of people donate continuously is high and the financial support is highly uncertain and volatile. But organizing a successful alternative project in a capitalist world requires continuity and stability. For-profit models can have all of the problems that regular corporate social media bring about: a usage fee excludes those who cannot pay, targeted advertising brings about problems of user exploitation and privacy-violating economic surveillance. Both advance the logic of capitalism and commodification that left-wing movements want to challenge. If there are one the one hand platforms that are accessible without payment and use targeted advertising (such as Facebook and Twitter) and on the other hand alternative platforms that charge usage fees, it could be that many users choose the ones, where they do not have to pay, which can further advance and sustain the monopolization of social media provision in favour of those that already dominate. Using for-profit models could also result in the substitution of activist logic by bureaucratic logic, which can not just result in an administered form of protest, but can also completely change the nature of political goals away from changing the system towards sustaining it. Once one runs a media company, there is a danger that filters such as appealing to mainstream audiences by not appearing radical, the advancement of entertainment and commerce instead of politics, the tabloidization of the media as well as appealing to and attracting advertisers set in and censor the kind of information that is visible in such a way that alternative politics is margin-alized and structurally discriminated.

Finally, there are also state-funded models. This could e.g. be a licence fee for Internet use that is used for providing subsidies for non-commercial Internet platforms and other non-commercial media projects. In the UK, the Media Reform Coalition suggests to introduce levies, "a surcharge or a tax on the revenues or profits of certain sections of the media industry" (CCMR 2011) paid by media corporations, such as providers of search and social media advertisers, news aggregators (Google, Yahoo, etc), Internet Service Providers, broadcasters, mobile phone operators and hardware companies, that are used for subsidizing local media cooperatives and public interest journalism (CCMR 2011).

The Occupy activists who completed the survey are rather sceptical of state funding. They mistrust the state and see it primarily as a coercive apparatus that tries to repress protest movements. Their own experiences with the police likely influence the way they assess the state and state politics. They tend to fear that state-organized subsidies for alternative media projects would give the state a new censorship tool and would make activists and their media too dependent on state support.

John Nichols and Robert W. McChesney (2010, see also McChesney and Nicholas 2010, 110f, 191) argue that state subsidies for the alternative press do not automatically result in censorship. The Nordic countries that tend to have a highly subsidized press would rank very high in rankings of civil liberties and press freedom. And indeed Finland, Norway, Denmark, Iceland and Sweden occupy the ranks 1, 3, 6, 9 and 10 in the 2013 World Press Freedom Index. But one nonetheless has to take seriously activists' fears and political opinion that alternative media's financial dependence on state subsidies provides the state with a powerful potential to censor and control alternative media. At the same time one should acknowledge that state censorship and control is not the automatic result of the implementation of state subsidies.

On the one hand there is truth in McChesney and Nichols' (2010,

112) argument that "fretting about government interference has grown increasingly dogmatic over the years". Especially conservatives who have neoliberal goals advance such opinions. McChesney and Nichols argue that democratizing the media system requires state support and state subsidies for the media. On the other hand one must understand that social movement-run media such as Occupii relate differently to the state than left-liberal media, such as the Guardian, because the Occupy movement has had intensive direct experience of violent state power. Here are some examples. On September 24th, 2011, NYPD officer Anthony Bologna attacked a group of young female Occupy activists with pepper spray. They were with the help of nets caught by the police when he carried out the assault. Activists recorded the incident and uploaded the video to YouTube.[23] Occupy Oakland occupied the Frank Ogawa Plaza in October 2011. On October 25th, the Oakland Police Department stormed the protest camp. The police fired beanbags and rubber bullets at the activists and injured several of them. Activist Scott Olsen suffered a skull fracture from a beanbag projectile shot by a police officer (Hurt Occupy Oakland protester was hit by a beanbag. *San Francisco Chronicle*, March 15, 2012[24]). On November 3rd, 2012, an officer fired a less-lethal round at Occupy activist Scott Campbell, who took a video of policemen (Experts: "Occupy" video shows excessive force. *CBS News*, November 9, 2011[25]). The shooting was documented by a video uploaded to YouTube.[26] Given the reality of police violence against the Occupy movement, it is no surprise that Occupy activists tend to be very sceptical about the state and any measures that could make social movement media dependent on state support.

The risk of state control could be somewhat limited by introducing media subsidies together with elements of participatory budgeting. John Nichols and Robert W. McChesney (2009) suggest a system, in which citizen tax credits subsidize alternative news projects. They argue in favour of giving citizens:

> an annual tax credit for the first $200 they spend on daily newspapers. The newspapers would have to publish at least five times per week and maintain a substantial 'news hole', say at least twenty-four broad pages each day, with less than 50 percent advertising. In effect, this means the government will pay for every citizen who so desires to get a free daily newspaper subscription, but the taxpayer gets to pick the newspaper – this is an indirect subsidy, because the government does not control who gets the money. This will buy time for our old media newsrooms – and for us citizens – to develop a plan to establish journalism in the digital era. We could see this evolving into a system to provide tax credits for online subscriptions as well (Nichols and McChesney 2009).

Some respondents noted that there are problems with all options. So for example one respondent argued: "I wish the donation-based model would work well, but the reality is that very few will (or can) donate. Similarly, few will pay a usage fee. If the state pays for social media then the state will feel entitled to monitor it. Sadly, this just leaves the first option but, of course, as you note there are serious problems with it too. I wish I knew the answer" (#333). For-profit models risk reproducing the business practices of the dominant social media platforms and to structurally censor critical thinking. Public funding models mediated by the state are unpopular among activists because they fear state surveillance and censorship. Many activists like voluntary donation models. At the same time donations are highly volatile and pose an insecure funding model. There seems to be no financial model without risks for alternative social media, which shows that the world of money negates and structurally limits the world of activism. Activism in a society that is governed by the logic of accumulation and money is facing structural limits.

If one takes the basic media reform funding idea of the UK Media Reform Coalition, namely to tax large media corporations and to levy this income into non-commercial media, and combines it with elements of participatory budgeting, which allows every citizens to donate a certain amount per year to a non-commercial media project, then elements of state action and civil society action could be combined: the power of the state would guarantee taxation of large media companies, the distribution of this income to media projects would however be decentralized and put in the hands of citizens.

Companies such as Google, Amazon and Starbucks had to appear before the UK Public Accounts Committee in late 2012 to answer questions about potential tax avoidance in the UK.[27] Amazon has 15 000 employees in the UK, but its headquarters are in Luxembourg, where it has just 500 employees.[28] In 2011, it generated revenues of £3.3 billion in the UK, but only paid £1.8 million corporation tax (0.05%).[29] Facebook paid £238 000 corporation tax on a UK revenue of £175 million (0.1%) in 2011.[30]

Google has its headquarters in Dublin, but employs around 700 people in the UK.[31] Google's Managing Director for the UK and Ireland, Matt Brittin, admitted that this choice of location is due to the circumstance that the corporation tax in Ireland is just 12.5% ,[32] whereas in the UK it was 26% in 2011.[33] Google had a UK turnover of £395 million in 2011, but only paid taxes of £6 million (1.5%).[34]

Google's CEO Eric Schmidt defended Google's practices by saying that the company in the UK "hired more than 2,000 employees", invested heavily, makes donations, empowers start-ups by its advertisement opportunities, "which is driving a lot of economic growth for the country."[35] When asked by the BCC about the circumstance that Google's UK employees and profits are being channelled through Ireland, Schmidt responded: "People we employ in Britain are certainly paying British taxes. … I think the most important thing to say about our taxes is that we fully comply with the law and obviously, should the law change, we'll comply with that as well."[36] The Public Accounts Committee said that Google, Starbucks and Amazon are "using the letter of tax laws both nationally and internationally to immorally minimise their tax obligations."[37] Google has a presence in the UK (Google UK Ltd), but profits made in the UK are channelled to Google Ireland Ltd. That "pays most of its turnover to an affiliate in Bermuda, which levies no income tax on foreign-controlled corporation."[38]

The basic mechanism of tax avoidance is enabled by legal loopholes that allow corporations that operate in several countries to declare taxes on profits made with operations in the UK in tax havens such as the Cayman Islands or Luxembourg, where they have headquarters or subsidiaries, but do not make the majority of their employees or revenues. So Schmidt is right that neoliberal governance regimes legally enable the tax avoidance practices of Google, Facebook, Amazon, Starbucks and other multinationals, which shows that neoliberalism operates both as corporate and state practice. At the same time, the example of Google shows that corporations and capitalists do not have morals. They will use every possibility they can find for maximizing and increasing profits. Capitalism knows no morals. It is an immoral economy and society.

Table 31 shows the worldwide 2011 revenues, profits, gross profit rates and the UK revenues and taxes of Amazon, Facebook and Google. It also estimates the profits of the three companies based on their global profit rates and shows an estimate of how large the tax income would have been if they had been taxed at a corporation tax rate of 28% of gross profits. The tax revenues would have been a total of £76 million. Given that the three companies paid combined taxes of £8 million, the estimated additional tax income would have been £68 million. Given that in 2011 there were 22.1 million households in the UK,[39] the corporation tax revenues from only these 3 companies could give each

	Amazon	Facebook	Google
UK Revenue 2011 (£)	3.3 bn	175 bn	395 mn
Worldwide Revenue 2011 (US$)	48.077 bn	3.711 bn	37.905 bn
Worldwide Profit before Taxes 2011 (US$)	934 mn	1.695 bn	12.326 bn
Gross Profit Rate 2011 (in % of revenue)	1.9%	45.7%	32.5%
Estimated Gross UK Profit, 2011 (£)	62.7 mn	80.0 mn	128.4 mn
UK Corporation Tax 2011 (£)	1.8 mn	238 000	6 mn
Estimated Tax Revenues at a Corporation Tax Rate of 28%	17.6 mn	22.4 mn	36.0 mn

Table 31: Financial figures and estimates for Amazon, Facebook and Google. Data sources: UK revenues: The Guardian Online, BBC Online; worldwide: Amazon SEC Filings 2012, Form 10-K; Google SEC Filings 2012, Form 10-K; Facebook SEC Filings 2013, Form 10-K

household £3 per year for participatory donations. One can imagine that given that this sum is already an estimated £3 per year if we only base the calculation on three companies, it could easily be £100-200 or more per household if all large corporations and therefore also all large media companies would be adequately taxed in the UK. It is absurd, but an actually existing ideology, that the UK government constantly talks about the necessity of austerity measures, cutting welfare benefits and state expenditures and that at the same time large corporations hardly pay taxes and the corporation tax has been reduced from 28% in 2010 to 21% in 2014. The best way for consolidating state households is to close tax loopholes, enforce the collection of corporation taxes and to increase corporation taxes. In the realm of media policies, taxing corporate media could enable social innovations that allow strengthening the media commons and the public character of the media by empowering citizen involvement in the form of participatory media budgeting that benefits alternative, non-commercial media. The UK's tradition in public service media could thereby be taken to a new level.

Robert McChesney and John Nichols (2010, 201) have introduced the idea of a Citizenship News Voucher, where every citizen "gets a $200 voucher she can use to donate money to any non-profit news medium of her choice". Media receiving voucher credits should according to McChesney (2012, 212) not be allowed to run advertisements. "The voucher system would provide a way for the burgeoning yet starving nonprofit digital news sector to become self-sufficient and have the funds to hire a significant number of full-time paid workers. ... Citizenship news vouchers would fill the Web with large amounts of professional-quality journalism and provide a genuine independent journalism sector" (McChesney 2012, 212, 214). Non-profit versions of Twitter, YouTube and Facebook run by activists could serve the purpose of advancing public political discourses and thereby the public sphere. Therefore a point can be made that a citizenship voucher system should not be restricted to news media, but extended to all forms of political and educational online platforms. McChesney and Nichols (2010, 209-211) suggest possible funding sources could include: a tax on commercial radio and television's use of the broadcast spectrum at a rate of 7% of their revenues, a tax of 5% on consumer electronics, a spectrum auction tax, a 2% sales tax on advertising and a 3 percent on ISP-cell phone users' monthly fees. The question that arises is why users of information and communication technologies (ICTs) should pay taxes rather than taxing the companies' revenues? One can make the argument that companies offset company taxation by increasing prices. But this can be hindered by rules that define how companies are allowed to set commodity prices. Other ideas for funding a participatory budgeting media donation system are to introduce a general tax paid by all for-profit companies, a general tax paid by all for-profit media, advertising and ICT companies and a special tax on wealth and high incomes.

The ideas for such systems are however far from perfect. If there is no legislation that allows such participatory budget media donations only for non-commercial media, it can happen that a large number of citizens donates to dominant commercial media that they like or to primarily entertainment-oriented and tabloid media. As a consequence, the dominance of specific corporate media and the privileging of entertainment and commerce over public interest media could be sustained. Participatory budgeting may then merely redistribute profits within the dominant media.

If there were, however, a legal regulation that guaranteed that participatory media budget donations can only be made to non-commercial, non-profit media, an unequal distribution between alternative media projects could still be the result of citizens preferring certain projects over others. This could result in the creation of monopolies or oligopolies within the alternative media sector. There is also the danger that dominant media corporations like News Corporation could create non-commercial media projects in order to exert political influence in the alternative media sector and instil right-wing politics and tabloid logic into it.

The survey also focused on the question if it is a good idea that social movements' media activists are paid or not. The question the survey asked was: "For protests, protest media are needed. Such media can only exist if people work for them as media activists. Often this work is voluntary and unpaid. Do you think it were a good idea to pay those people who take care of the press/news work, websites, software, live video streams, newspapers?" The answer options were:

- No, I think social movement media work should always be voluntary and unpaid.
- Yes, I think one should find ways for paying these people because I believe this can improve a protest movement's visibility in the public.
- Other (please specify below).

Table 32 summarizes the analysis of the answers.

Answer	Frequency	Share (%)
No, it should always be voluntary	101	35.8%
Yes. I think one should find ways for paying these people	105	37.2%
Other	64	22.7%
Do not know	12	4.3%

Table 32: Respondents' views on the question if media work in social movements should be paid, N=282

Almost equal shares of the respondents argued that social movement media work should be paid (37.2%) or not (35.8%). 22.7% held another opinion, often stressing that this is a very difficult issue and that they are undecided on it.

Here some of the answers indicating that media work for social movements should be remunerated:

- "Myself and my colleagues work night and day at great personal cost. If this movement is to continue, people need to be able to draw a living wage from their work" (#16).
- "I believe people should be rewarded for work contributing to the commons" (#41).
- "Unpaid work limits who can be involved and for how long" (#233).

- "It concerns us all - I don' t want any money for the time I spend with my grandchildren - and that's almost the same thing" (#301).

Some stressed potential risks of remuneration:

- "The more you move to concretize and fund the more you become a bureaucracy, an NGO. It is the freshness, and passion of the volunteer that is needed in the midst of revolution. It keeps all talents equal. If you pay them then everyone should be paid. Activism should always be part of ones life, not something they get paid for. We now see the commodification of activism and it just is a wet blanket on real change. Then everyone gets bought into the system" (#321).
- "It is a free protest, and if we pay them (Other than real expenses) it will lead to what is going on in all our US government operations" (#56).

Others stressed that it is a question that is difficult for them to answer or that they have different preferences:

- "Micro-donations: If EACH Occupier had their own page that showed what they do and each thing they do was somehow highlighted (by the Occupier, our media, social platforms, working group reports etc.) then EACH could be almost self-funded based on what they do OR/AND each working group, project etc. had a micro-funding option (flattr.com or similar or better still, our own) then that group or activity could be rewarded/applauded and the funds divided by the group" (#2).
- "Highly contextual – sometimes unpaid volunteers are put off when they get organised by paid employees of an NGO – but in some scenarios where you need a difficult or

technical task performed to a very high standard, paying professionals for help might be perfectly sensible. Again, there is an ecology of social movements – some NGOs are run like corporations which might not appeal to some but arguably means they perform some kinds of work that grass-roots volunteer groups cannot. Both are needed" (#11).

- "Very difficult question. Pros and cons on both sides. People should be able to get a fair wage for ethical work that they do ... but if some people are getting paid that tends to create hierarchies. Perhaps, if people form genuine non-hierarchical ethical co-operatives or collectives and find a way to bring in enough ethical funds (preferably on donation or crowdfunded basis) to pay themselves equitably ... that might be ok" (#13).

- "This is a huge discussion within Occupy LA. Those who are paid are often not trusted. Personally I think if someone gets a small amount of money to help them continue to be involved it can be good. And ultimately if someone finds a new passion and can then make a living doing it - that's part of the personal transformation Occupy is about. Some of our streamers are now actual journalists. But it is tricky and complicated" (#55).

- "If there's money, pay them if it takes a lot of time. If not then those who want to will do it for free, willingly" (#61).

- "I think they should be voluntary and unpaid but i think efforts should be made to provide meals, housing and any other basic needs for the individuals to compensate for the time they put into it" (#76).

- "Having both citizen journalist and paid journalist ensures the well roundedness of this media. I support both" (#360).

- "This is a hard one. I am a live streamer and I do this for free, for the movement. But I rely on donations to keep up on bills that pile up due to live stream costs" (#241).

- "If they are paid it opens it up to abuse (what is fair compensation for time/effort?). Better to reimburse for expenses and minimum fee per activity if funds available" (#272).
- "Modestly compensate when and where possible; however, don't compromise the ideals to sponsorships. It could, all too easily, turn the Occupy into just another purchased vote and voice; yet another sell-out to silence an actual need/s" (#323).
- "We do need to create a new co-operative society where money is not at the center of everything!" (#347).

The final survey question was aimed at those who in the preceding question had answered that social movement media activists should be paid. It asked: "You have indicated that you think the work of media activists in protest movements should be paid. What do you think is the best way for being able to pay them?" Table 33 displays the results of the analysis of the respondents' answers. The most prominent option is to collect voluntary donations, followed by running non-profit cooperatives that sell memberships.

There is no clear majority on the question if social media activists should be paid or not. On the one hand, respondents stress that media activism takes a lot of time and that paying media activists would therefore improve the movements' communication possibilities. On the other hand, they point out that there is a danger of becoming a bureaucratic NGO with reformist goals and that activism is commodified, although the movement questions the logic of commodification. Those who are in favour of paying activists tend to favour voluntary donation models.

Answer	Frequency	Share (%)
To collect voluntary donations from activists and those who sympathise with the movement.	44	44.4%
The state should provide public funding for social movement's media projects.	11	11.1%%
Social movements should turn their media projects into a profitable business/company that uses advertising as business model.	3	3.0%
Social movements should operate their media as a self-managed non-commercial and non-profit cooperative that sells memberships, but is not allowed to make a profit.	27	27.3%
Social movements should operate their media by selling access to these media, but only for funding employees and not for making a monetary profit.	9	9.1%
Other. Please specify.	5	5.1%

Table 33: Answers of respondents, who think that media activists should be paid, to the question how resources for such payments should be mobilized, N=99

8. Conclusion: Activism and the Media in a World of Antagonisms

On September 19th, 2011, the alternative news service Democracy Now! reported on Occupy Wall Street.[40] The broadcast reports were activist-centred and gave voice to activists such as Mary Ellen Marino, who was interviewed and said: "I came because I'm upset with the fact that the bailout of Wall Street didn't help any of the people holding mortgages. All of the money went to Wall Street, and none of it went to Main Street". The studio guests were David Graeber (anthropologist and Occupy activist) and Nathan Schneider (editor of the blog "Waging nonviolence"). On November 18th 2012, policeman John Pike pepper-sprayed non-violent student protestors who conducted a sit-in at the University of California's campus in Davis. Activists filmed the incident and uploaded the video to YouTube. "One of the main features of the Occupy movements was having media on hand to document their activities and those of police brutality" (Kellner 2012, 5909). The hacker group Anonymous found out private details of John Pike and posted them online together with the video.[41] YouTube, after some time deleted the video, saying: "This video is no longer available due to a copyright claim by Thomas Fowler". News Corporation's commercial TV channel Fox reported about the pepper spray attack on November 21st. Bill O'Reilly and Megan Kelly discussed the attack: "First of all: pepper spray. ... It's a food production essentially. ... They just wanted them to get out of there, stop blocking what they were blocking. ... And it is a crime ... because they were posing, you know, a sit-in, a student protest. ... It looks like the students were failing to disperse. ... The police chief has been placed on administrative leave, right? For obeying orders! Isn't that nice?"[42] Fox News produced a report that presented Occupiers as morons by showing highly edited excerpts from interviews with activists that were interlaced with excerpts from movies and focused especially on one activist, who said that marijuana should be legalized.[43]

This example shows the contradictory character of contemporary media: Various media relate to social movements in different ways. Alternative media, such as Democracy Now!, tend to share activists' position and give space to the expression of their views. Right-wing mainstream media, such as Fox News, in contrast try to present a very different picture of social movements, presenting them as stupid, violent, plan- and strategy-less and showing sympathy with police violence. In contrast, other mainstream media, such as Al Jazeera and the Guardian, reported in a relatively sympathetic manner on Occupy Wall Street (Graeber 2013, 62). Commercial social media such as YouTube are simultaneously spaces of publication and censorship of activists' voices and views. Activists hardly get the opportunity to present their views in commercial right-wing mainstream media, interviews are manipulated and edited in a manner that allows ridiculing the movement. In the case of Occupy, Democracy Now! and Fox related to the movement in contradictory ways. There are conflicts and contradictions between different type of media and between specific media organizations. These relations are shaped by power: whereas Democracy Now!'s website is the world's 23 039th most viewed site, Fox News' site is ranked in position 160 (alexa.com, December 2nd, 2012). Visibility on the Internet and audience reach are important aspects of communication power and have to do with the budgets and reputation of media. Commercial media that base their revenues on advertisements have advantages, whereas non-commercial media that depend on donations and foundations are facing communicative inequality. The YouTube video that was uploaded on November 18th, 2011,[44] received 1 825 590 views until April 28th, 2013 (05:49 a.m. BST; = a period of 527 days). These are on average 3464 viewings per day. In contrast, Fox News' prime-time ratings were around 1.9 million viewers per day in 2011.[45] This means that Fox News has the power to reach more viewers in one day than a citizen journalist's clip reaches on YouTube over one and a half years. The net effect is that the right-wing comments and manipulated videos that Fox News showed about Occupy reached a broader viewing than the activist-oriented reporting of Democracy Now! and the uncommented footage available on YouTube. This circumstance shows that how the media relate to social movements is shaped by contradictions that are embedded into power structures and power asymmetries. Alternative media and alternative views are, due to the structure of the media landscape in capitalism, at a disadvantage and are facing structural communication inequalities. Activists make use of commercial online media such as YouTube that can potentially reach a broad public, but that they do not control themselves.

The example shows the contradictory character of media power in capitalist societies. This study showed that digital and social media have a multidimensional contradictory character in social movements:

- *The Occupy movement is an antagonist of the logic of commodification:* It negates and struggles against the commodification of the commons and for a society that is based on the logic of the commons.
- *The contradiction between protest communication and communication control on social media*: There is a contradiction between social media's opportunities for supporting protest movements' networking, mobilization and bypassing the mainstream media and the risks surveillance as evidenced by the existence of the PRISM system, censorship, separation from street protests, infiltration by the police and secret services, corporate control and a stratified visibility and attention economy.

- *The duality of media activists and other activists*: Activists tend to be highly media-savvy and use various media for information, communication, coordination and mobilization. There are on the one hand activists who occasionally use social media for social movement communication (e.g. posting announcements on Facebook or Twitter) and a smaller group of social media activists who run live feeds, alternative news services, program software, administer or design websites, blog frequently, shoot and share videos, etc.
- *The dialectic of online and offline protest communication*: Activists use multiple online and offline channels for obtaining information, discussing protests and trying to mobilize others. Online communication and face-to-face communication for these purposes tend to mutually reinforce each other.
- *The antagonism of public communication and communication control on commercial social media*: There is a fundamental contradiction between commercial social media's potential that activists can use for reaching out to a broad public on the one hand and the risks that commercial platforms deliberately or algorithmically censor activists' communications and that the police monitors or infiltrates social movements on these platforms.
- *The antagonism of alternative social media's critical voice and autonomy on the one hand and resource precarity on the other hand*: There is a contradiction between non-commercial social media's non-profit organization model that fits the goals of the Occupy movement and reduces the probability of censorship and surveillance on the one hand, and, on the other, the problems of resource precarity and low public outreach that often characterize such platforms. Alternative social media provide autonomy for critical voices, but often suffer from a lack of public attention and

visibility. They are confronted with a structural form of censorship and discrimination immanent in capitalism that benefits large, resourceful, profitable, visible corporate media at the expense of alternative media.

- *The contradiction of for-profit and non-profit (social) media*: For-profit (social) media tend to accumulate money, users/audience members, visibility, attention, reputation, political influence, whereas the latter tend to lack such resources and have to struggle against this condition.

- *The contradiction of voluntariness and vulnerability of social media-donation models*: Activists tend to favour voluntary donation models for organizing alternative media. A significant share of them is willing to donate on average €10 per month for such media. Voluntary donations are at the same time a vulnerable and potentially instable source of funding.

- *The contradiction of state-funded stability and control of alternative social media*: State-organized funding could provide a more stable source of funding, but activists are highly critical of such models because they fear that such funding could reduce their autonomy and the state could more easily police, monitor or censor their communications.

- *The contradiction of for-profit organization and loss of autonomy*: For-profit models can increase the visibility and the user base of alternative media, but risk the loss of autonomy and critical analysis due to corporate pressures.

- *The contradiction of the stability of paid media activism and the logic of bureaucratization and commodification*: Paying media activists could improve social movements' communication possibilities but could also at the same time turn movements into bureaucratic NGOs with reformist goals and commodify activism, although the movement questions the logic of commodification.

Being an Occupy activist means helping to awaken the dialectic of capitalist society. Although society has been highly antagonistic in the past decades, which expressed itself in high inequalities and risks, these antagonisms have often not been clearly articulated in the political public sphere. The Occupy movement emerged in a situation of crisis, in which capitalism's antagonisms manifest themselves evidently. It is a movement that makes capitalism's inherent antagonisms visible and an issue of debate in the public sphere. Being an activist in a highly mediated society brings both opportunities and risks, which reflects the antagonistic character of the media in capitalist society. Activists are permanently confronted with having to manage the contradictions of communication and control, critical voice and the challenge of resource mobilization, voluntariness and vulnerability, non-profit and for-profit, commercial and non-commercial that shape the media landscape in capitalism. Being an activist means not just to confronting the socio-economic and political inequalities that capitalism is producing, but to also confronting the antagonisms and inequalities that shape the media system in capitalist society. Democratic societies give voice, power, visibility and wealth to everyone. Many contemporary social movements are political screams for change that do not accept inequalities and want to see transformations. A society's degree of democracy is expressed in the way it deals with, supports or limits the activities of protest movements. Occupy activists struggle for a democratic and just society. At the same time they use corporate social media such as Facebook that exploit users' work and collaborate with the police in the PRISM system for monitoring citizens, which undermines freedom of speech, thought and assembly. Powerful non-commercial alternative media platforms are urgently needed in order to make activists independent from corporate and state control. Media activists make use of commercial and non-commercial media for contesting the inequalities of society. They are, in these media struggles, confronted with the inequalities of the capitalist media system and contest the structures of this very system. The Occupy movement expresses, through its struggles, that another society is needed and possible. Another media system is possible because it is needed. A public service and commons-based Internet is possible because it is needed. Such an Internet communalizes the ownership of platforms and thereby helps establishing truly social media that benefit not just an elite, but can advance the public good and the common interests of all.

Endnotes

1. Occupy Wall Street, Principles of Solidarity, http://www.nycga.net/category/assemblies/minutes/community-discussions/
2. http://briandeer.com/social/thatcher-society.htm
3. http://www.democracynow.org/blog/2013/5/22/dissent_or_terror_counter_terrorism_apparatus_used_to_monitor_occupy_movement_nationwide
4. http://www.democracynow.org/2013/5/22/editor_of_the_progressive_calls_for
5. http://www.guardian.co.uk/world/2013/jun/06/us-tech-giants-nsa-data, http://www.theguardian.co.uk/world/2013/jul/31/nsa-top-secret-program-online-data
6. http://www.bbc.co.uk/news/world-us-canada-22809541
7. http://www.guardian.co.uk/world/2013/jun/17/edward-snowden-nsa-files-whistleblower
8. http://www.guardian.co.uk/world/2013/jun/08/nsa-boundless-informant-global-datamining#zoomed-picture
9. http://www.guardian.co.uk/world/interactive/2013/jun/06/verizon-telephone-data-court-order
10. http://www.cbsnews.com/8301-205_162-57588319/google-ceo-larry-page-issues-statement-on-prism/
11. https://www.facebook.com/zuck/posts/10100828955847631
12. http://www.guardian.co.uk/world/2013/jun/07/prism-tech-giants-shock-nsa-data-mining
13. http://blog.aol.com/2013/06/07/aol-statement-regarding-nsa-prism/
14. http://www.guardian.co.uk/world/2013/jun/09/edward-snowden-nsa-whistleblower-surveillance
15. http://fuchs.uti.at/389/
16. http://www.guardian.co.uk/uk/2013/jun/25/undercover-police-domestic-extremism-unit?INTCMP=SRCH
17. http://www.guardian.co.uk/uk/2013/jun/21/gchq-cables-

secret-world-communications-nsa

18. http://progressive.org/spying-on-ccupy-activists
19. http://projects.washingtonpost.com/top-secret-america /articles/a-hidden-world-growing-beyond-control/
20. http://investors.boozallen.com/sec.cfm
21. There are of course also ecological crises that can threaten the existence of humankind. For social theory, the question is how nature relates to society. Humans have to enter into a metabolic relation with nature in order to survive. They have to appropriate parts of nature and change it with their activities in order to produce use-values that serve human needs. This means that the process, where the interaction of nature and society is directly established, takes place in the economy. We therefore do not discern ecological crises separately, but see them as one specific subform of economic crises.
22. Data sources: http://www.alexa.com/topsites, http://www. internetworldstats.com/
23. http://www.youtube.com/watch?v=erfxKBSsIJE
24. http://www.sfgate.com/crime/article/Hurt-Occupy-Oakland-protester-was-hit-by-beanbag-3408025.php
25. http://www.cbsnews.com/8301-201_162-57321440/experts-occupy-vid-shows-excessive-force/
26. http://www.youtube.com/watch?v=I0pX9LeE-g8
27. Starbucks, Google and Amazon grilled over tax avoidance. *BBC Online.* November 12, 2012. http://www.bbc.co.uk/news /business-20288077
28. ibid.
29. Amazon: £7bn sales, no UK corporation tax. *The Guardian Online.* April 4, 2012. http://www.guardian.co.uk/technology /2012/apr/04/amazon-british-operation-corporation-tax. Google, Amazon, Starbucks: The rise of "tax sharing". BBC Online. December 4, 2012. http://www.bbc.co.uk/news /magazine-20560359

30. Should we boycott the tax-avoiding companies? *The Guardian Online.* Shortcuts Blog. October 17, 2012. http://www.guardian.co.uk/business/shortcuts/2012/oct/17/b oycotting-tax-avoiding-companies

31. Google and auditor recalled by MPs to answer tax questions. *The Guardian Online.* May 1, 2013. http://www.guardian.co .uk/technology/2013/may/01/google-parliament-tax-questions

32. Starbucks, Google and Amazon grilled over tax avoidance. *BBC Online.* November 12, 2012. http://www.bbc.co.uk/ news/business-20288077

33. In the UK, the main rate of corporation tax that applies for profits exceeding £1 500 000, was reduced from 28% in 2010 to 26% in 2011, 24% in 2012, 23% in 2013 and 21% in 2014.

34. Ibid.

35. Google boss defends UK tax record to BBC. *BBC Online.* April 22, 2013. http://www.bbc.co.uk/news/business-2224 5770

36. ibid.

37. Eric Schmidt defends Google tax affairs, saying firm was key to UK growth. *The Guardian Online.* April 22, 2013. http:// www.guardian.co.uk/technology/2013/apr/22/eric-schmidt-google-tax-affairs-growth

38. Special Report: How Google UK clouds its tax liabilities. *Reuters UK.* May 1, 2013. http://www.reuters.com/article /2013/05/01/us-tax-uk-google-specialreport-idUSBRE9 4005P20130501

39. Department for Communities and Local Government, Household interim projections, 2011 to 2021. https:// www.gov.uk/government/publications/household-interim-projections-2011-to-2021-in-england

40. http://www.democracynow.org/2011/9/19/occupy_wall_ street_thousands_march_in

41. Original URL: http://www.youtube.com/watch?v=BjnR

7xET7Uo
42. http://tpmdc.talkingpointsmemo.com/2011/11/fox-news-on-uc-davis-pepper-spraying-its-a-food-product-essentially.php?ref=fpnewsfeed
43. http://www.youtube.com/watch?v=Zd8o_yqqo9o
44. http://www.youtube.com/watch?v=6AdDLhPwpp4
45. http://stateofthemedia.org/2012/cable-cnn-ends-its-ratings-slide-fox-falls-again/

References

Aouragh, Miriyam. 2012. Social media, mediation and the Arab revolutions. *tripleC: Communication, Capitalism & Critique: Open Access Journal for a Global Sustainable Information Society* 10 (2): 518-536.

Atton, Chris. 2002. *Alternative media*. London: Sage.

Babbie, Earl R. 2010. *The practice of social research*. London. Cengage Learning.

Badiou, Alain. 2012. *The rebirth of history. Times of riots and uprisings*. London: Verso.

Bennett, W. Lance and Alexandra Segerberg. 2012. The logic of connective action. *Information, Communication & Society* 15 (5): 739-768.

Bennett, W. Lance and Alexandra Segerberg. 2013. *The logic of connective action. Digital media and the personalization of contentious politics*. Cambridge: Cambridge University Press.

Bryman, Alan. 2012. *Social research methods*. Oxford: Oxford University Press. 4th edition.

Castells, Manuel. 1996. *The rise of the network society*. Malden, MA: Blackwell.

Castells, Manuel. 1997. *The power of identity*. Malden, MA: Blackwell.

Castells, Manuel. 2012. *Networks of outrage and hope. Social movements in the Internet age*. Cambridge: Polity Press.

Chomsky, Noam. 2012. *Occupy*. London: Penguin.

Co-ordinating Committee for Media Reform (CCMR). 2011. *Funding models for news in the public interest*. http://www.mediareform.org.uk/wordpress/wp-content/uploads/2013/04/Funding-models-for-news-in-the-public-interest.pdf

Dean, Jodi. 2012. *The communist horizon*. London: Verso.

Duménil, Gérard and Dominique Lévy. 2011. *The crisis of neoliberalism*. Cambridge, MA: Harvard University Press.

Foster, John Bellamy and Robert McChesney. 2012. *The endless crisis. How Monopoly-finance capital produces stagnation and upheaval from the USA to China*. New York: Monthly Review Press.

Fuchs, Christian. 2006. The self-organization of social movements. *Systemic Practice and Action Research* 19 (1): 101-137.

Fuchs, Christian. 2008. *Internet and society. Social theory in the information age*. New York: Routledge.

Fuchs, Christian. 2010a. Alternative media as critical media. *European Journal of Social Theory* 13 (2): 173-192.

Fuchs, Christian. 2010b. Social software and web 2.0: their sociological foundations and implications. In *Handbook of research on web 2.0, 3.0, and X.0: technologies, business, and social applications. Volume II*, ed. San Murugesan, 764-789. Hershey, PA: IGI-Global.

Fuchs, Christian. 2012a. Behind the news. Social media, riots, and revolutions. *Capital & Class* 36 (3): 383-391.

Fuchs, Christian. 2012b. Some reflections on Manuel Castells' book "Networks of outrage and hope. Social movements in the Internet age". *tripleC: Communication, Capitalism & Critique: Journal for a Global Sustainable Information Society* 10 (2): 775-797.

Fuchs, Christian. 2014a. *Digital labour and Karl Marx*. New York: Routledge.

Fuchs, Christian. 2014b. *Social media. A critical introduction*. London: Sage.

Garnham, Nicholas. 1990. *Capitalism and communication*. London: Sage.

Gerbaudo, Paolo. 2012. *Tweets and the streets. Social media and contemporary activism*. London: Pluto Press.

Ghonim, Wael. 2012. *Revolution 2.0. The power of the people is greater than the people in power. A memoir*. New York: Houghton Mifflin Hartcourt.

Gladwell, Malcolm. 2010. Small change. Why the revolution will not be tweeted. *The New Yorker* October 2010: 42-49.

Gladwell, Malcolm and Clay Shirky. 2011. From innovation to revolution. Do social media make protests possible? *Foreign Affairs* 90 (2): 153-154.

Golding, Peter, and Graham Murdock. 1978. Theories of communication and theories of society. *Communication Research* 5 (3): 339on Re

Goodwin, Jeff. 2001. *No other way out. States and revolutionary movements, 1945-1991*. Cambridge: Cambridge University Press.

Graeber, David. 2013. *The democracy project. A history, a crisis, a movement*. London: Penguin.

Habermas, Jürgen. 1989. *The structural transformation of the public sphere*. Cambridge, MA: MIT Press.

Hardt, Michael and Antonio Negri. 2012. *Declaration*. Kindle edition.

Harvey, David. 1990. *The condition of postmodernity*. Malden, MA: Blackwell.

Harvey, David. 2010. *The enigma of capital*. London: Profile Books.

Harvey, David. 2011a. The urban roots of financial crisis: Reclaiming the city for anti-capitalist struggle. *Socialist Register* 48: 1-25.

Harvey, David. 2011b. The enigma of capital and the crisis this time. In *Business as usual. The roots of the financial meltdown*, ed. Graig Calhoun and Georgi Derluguian, 89-112, New York: New York University Press.

Harvey, David. 2012. *Rebel cities. From the right to the city to the urban revolution*. London: Verso.

Hayes, Ben. 2009. *NeoConOpticon. The EU security-industrial complex*. Amsterdam: Transnational Institute.

Hodai, Beau. 2013. *Dissent or terror*. Madison, WI: Center for Media and Democracy/DBA Press.

Hofkirchner, Wolfgang. 2013. *Emergent information. A Unified Theory of Information framework*. Singapore: World Scientific.

Juris, Jeffrey S. 2012. Reflections on #occupy everywhere: social media, public space, and emerging logics of aggregation. *American Ethnologist* 39 (2): 259-279.

Kellner, Douglas. 2012. *Media spectacle and insurrection, 2011. From the Arab uprisings to Occupy Everywhere.* London: Bloomsbury. Kindle edition.

Kliman, Andrew. 2012. *The failure of capitalist production. Underlying causes of the great recession.* New York: Pluto.

Lapavitsas, Costas et al. 2012. *Crisis in the Eurozone.* London: Verso.

Marx, Karl. 1863. *Theories of surplus value. Books I, II, and III.* Amherst, NY: Prometheus Books.

Marx, Karl. 1867. *Capital. Volume 1.* London: Penguin.

Mason, Paul. 2012. *Why it's kicking off everywhere. The new global revolutions.* London: Verso.

McChesney, Robert W. 2012. *Digital disconnect. How capitalism is turning the Internet against democracy.* New York: The New Press.

McChesney, Robert W. and John Nichols. 2010. *The death and life of American journalism. The media revolution that will begin the world again.* New York: Nation Books.

McNally, David. 2011. *Global slump. The economics and politics of crisis and resistance.* Oakland: PM Press.

Mills, C. Wright. 1956. *The power elite.* Oxford: Oxford University Press.

Morozov, Evgeny. 2009. The brave new world of slacktivism. http://neteffect.foreignpolicy.com/posts/2009/05/19/the_brave _new_world_of_slacktivism

Morozov, Evgeny. 2010. *The net delusion. How not to liberate the world.* London: Allen Lane.

Morozov, Evgeny. 2013. *To save everything, click here. Technology, solutionism and the urge to fix problems that don't exist.* London: Allen Lane.

Mosco, Vincent. 2009. *The political economy of communication.*

London: Sage. 2nd edition.

Mosco, Vincent and Catherine McKercher. 2009. *The laboring of communication. Will knowledge workers of the world unite?* Lanham, MD: Lexington Books.

Nichols, John and Robert W. McChesney. 2009. The death and life of great American newspapers. *The Nation*, April 6, 2009. http://www.thenation.com/article/death-and-life-great-american-newspapers

Nichols, John and Robert W. McChesney. 2010. How to save journalism. *The Nation*, January 25, 2010. http://www.thenation.com/article/how-save-journalism

Punch, Keith F. 2005. *Introduction to social research. Quantitative and qualitative approaches*. London: Sage.

Resnick, Stephen and Rick Wolff. 2010. The economic crisis. A Marxian interpretation. *Rethinking Marxism* 22 (2): 170-186.

Sandoval, Marisol and Christian Fuchs. 2010. Towards a critical theory of alternative media. *Telematics and Informatics* 27 (2): 141-150.

Sullivan, Andrew. 2009. The revolution will be twittered. http://www.theatlantic.com/daily-dish/archive/2009/06/the-revolution-will-be-twittered/200478/_

Žižek, Slavoj. 2012. *The year of dreaming dangerously*. London: Verso.